Inspecting Commercial Kitchen Systems

Fifth Edition

Inspecting Commercial Kitchen Systems

Published by:

Phillip Ackland Holdings Ltd.

P. O. Box 856, Summerland, B.C. Canada V0H 1Z0

packland@shaw.ca   www.philackland.com

National Library of Canada Cataloguing in Publication Data

Ackland, Phil, 1949-

    Inspection manual for commercial kitchen exhaust systems manual

Rev. Ed.

Previously published under title: Phil Ackland's Commercial kitchen

    Exhaust systems manual: Restaurant and Inspectors' edition.

    Includes bibliographical references.

    ISBN-10: 1479125245, ISBN-13: 978-1479125241

    1. Kitchens--Equipment and supplies--Inspection. 2. Exhaust systems--Inspection. I. Commercial Kitchen Exhaust Institute (Summerland, B.C.) II. Phil Ackland's Commercial Kitchen exhaust systems manual. III. Title.

    TX656.A25 2001   697.9'2   C2001-902245-X

About the Author and Special Contributors

Phil Ackland

Phil Ackland has been in the commercial kitchen field for over 45 years. He is a principle member of the NFPA 96 Committee.

He has written numerous articles and a series of books on the subjects of installing, inspecting and servicing commercial kitchen exhaust and extinguishing systems (referenced in NFPA 96 and 921).

Philip Ackland Holdings Ltd has been ISO 9001 Certified. They offer training to fire and building inspectors, investigators, the insurance profession, and contract cleaners.

Phil Ackland and Associates provides a variety of qualified experts for consultation and technical support services to fire investigators and attorneys on kitchen system related insurance liability claims. He has assisted a number of authorities having jurisdiction develop and implement Certification Programs for inspectors and exhaust cleaners.

Lemuel L. (Speedy) Laster

Speedy's background was in welding and fabricating. He also served as Plant Manager and Safety Coordinator for a multinational chemical manufacturing company in North Georgia.

He founded Speedy Clean LLC. Speedy Clean is full service power washing company with the primary focus on Commercial Kitchen Exhaust cleaning. Mr. Laster is a member of the National Fire Protection Association (N.F.P.A.).

Mr. Laster joined Phil Ackland Inc. in 2007 as an Instructor; training individuals for commercial kitchen exhaust cleaning. In November 2008, Mr. Laster received his credentials from Mr. Ackland to teach the Fire Inspectors Course and has taught the Inspectors course at numerous locations across America and the Orient. He also provides hands-on inspection services.

Don Stewart

Don Stewart is a kitchen fire suppression systems expert with over 30 years of experience. His area of expertise is in the design and installation of Class II kitchen suppression systems. Over the last 10 years he has consulted to authorities having jurisdiction, insurance companies and fire protection companies on the design, installation, maintenance and compliance to manufacturers' guidelines on both wet and dry chemical kitchen fire suppression systems.

He conducts fire investigations and provides litigation support testimony to fire incidents in commercial kitchen fire suppression systems.

He is factory trained and certified by many fire suppression manufacturers including Ansul, Chemetron, FSI, General, Kidde, Range Guard and System Master. Don Stewart is a licensed sprinkler contractor in the state of Michigan; and holds engineered, pre-engineered and fire extinguisher licenses in the state of Illinois.

Mark Finck

Professional with extensive experience in all aspects of cooking equipment development, performance, application, and efficiencies. Comprehensive background in Quick Service Restaurants (QSR) kitchen operations, food chemistry, manufacturing and agency codes.

Subject matter expert (SME) in Ventilation, Commercial Ovens and Flame Broilers. Adept at optimizing global equipment specifications generating significant cost savings and promoting innovative solutions in complex environments.

- Rapidly analyze food preparation and food service system operations – KitchenologyTM
- Develop new innovative patentable technologies, saving energy and cost.
- Frequent industry key note speaker at large conferences.

Acknowledgments

We would like to take this opportunity to thank these individuals and companies.

Special Thanks to:

- **George Zawacki** for the insight and technical assistance with the pre-occupancy, engineering and ASHRAE technical information.

- **Halton** for use of their photograph on our manual cover.

- **Steve Bradbury** for all his pictures and expertise in the area of water wash hoods and fire systems.

- **Tamora Davy** for her concise and exceptional focus on the editing and proofing, as well as the ability to store all those pictures in her mind for convenient recall.

- **Daryl Mirza** of National Fire Service, for many of the photographs in the manual and for his expertise and financial contributions to the video that now make this a complete educational package.

- **Scott Stookey**, ICC Senior Technical Staff Production Development, for review and development of the IMC and IFC referenced sections.

- **Mark Conroy,** Engineer with Brooks Equipment Company, for providing editorial comments on 2014 NFPA 96 Standards. Copyright material used with permission of Brooks Equipment Company, Charlotte, NC.

Individuals:

Gary Barros, Barney Besal, Alan Breitenfeldt, Hugh Byrom. Larry Capalbo, Tom Carter, Russell Clark, Lee DeVito, Rod Getz, Ted Giles, Troy Hassman, Mike and Robert Hinderliter, Kevin Jones, Tim Kelly, Jeff Kennedy, Gary Kreller, Tony Lombardo, Shaun Ray, Diane MacDonald, Robert Niemeier, Dave Russell, Greg Thompson, Doc Reisman, Jim Roberts, Greg Seddon, Rory Wilson, Bill Wesche, Elwood Willey

Companies:

3M Corporation, Ansul, Bryan Exhaust Service, Component Hardware Group, Craig West Associates, Deluxe Cleaning Systems of Fort Worth, DPW Services, Ducts Unlimited, Fire Commissioners Office of British Columbia, Fire Prevention Officers Association of British Columbia, FirePro, Flame Gard, Gaylord, Giles Food Service Equipment, Greenheck, Kidde-Fenwal Inc., McDonald's Corporation, Master Air, Metal Fab, National Fire Protection Association, National Fire Service, Power Washers of North America, Quest Ventilator Company, Restaurant Services, Inc, SMACNA, Selkirk Metalbestos, Summerland Fire Department, Supreme Fan Products, Thermal Ceramics, VentMaster, Video Innovations.

Table of Contents

Phil Ackland's Inspection Manual for Commercial Kitchen Systems

Flame in Fryer

Chapter One – General

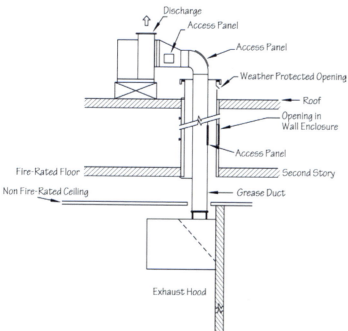

Components of a typical exhaust system

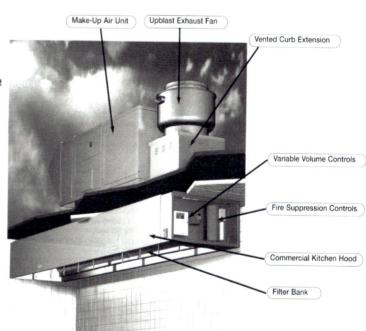

A general view of a commercial kitchen ventilation system.
Courtesy of Greenheck.

General

Commercial Kitchen Ventilation (CKV)

Originally cooking ventilation was nothing more than a hole in the roof or chimney under which fire was used to cook food indoors. If it got hot from lack of air, a door or window was opened.

Gradually it was realized that more cooking appliances could be added and major cooking operations could take place by including a hood to capture the greasy air, a duct to direct it out of the building, and a fan to pull it through the duct.

Properly designed and balanced commercial kitchen ventilation (CKV) systems can provide thousands of dollars a year in energy savings. Over the past 50-plus years, the growth of restaurants and commercial cooking operations has grown phenomenally. With this growth has come greater understanding of the importance of a healthy and safe kitchen environment. The CKV system contributes to that environment.

Radiant heat and thermal energy from the convective plume created by the appliances is removed by the CKV system. Properly balanced (conditioned) ventilation ensures that the kitchen staff and other occupants are provided with clean (makeup) air to replace the contaminated cooking (exhaust) air.

Beyond healthy air movement, the removal of combustible grease contaminants from the cooking processes prevents fire conditions from developing within the system.

Because combustible grease vapors will condense and accumulate within the exhaust system, it is necessary for the exhaust section of the CKV system to be constructed and installed in a way to withstand the possibility of an internal fire. Additionally, fire-extinguishing equipment is housed in the CKV to extinguish potential fires that can take place in appliances and within the exhaust system.

It is the relationship between the appliances and exhaust system, and the potential for fire that is the main theme of this publication.

> *NFPA 96, Section 11.1.1: Exhaust systems shall be operated whenever cooking equipment is turned on.*

Note: The expression "Commercial Kitchen Ventilation" or "CKV" defines both the exhaust <u>and</u> the air makeup and/or return air -- Heating, Ventilation, Air Conditioning (HVAC) system. The primary focus of this manual is to provide information on the exhaust portions of the CKV system.

Air Movement

Regarding kitchen exhaust systems, the example is drawn between water running out of a bathtub and air exhausting out of a kitchen system. The drain of the tub has to handle all the water coming in; the same is true of the exhaust system. To prevent the hood from filling up with smoke and grease vapors, at least an equal (or greater) amount of air must be "drained" out. As all buildings and exhaust systems are designed differently, the various airflows (both exhaust and makeup) need to be accommodated in a number of different ways.

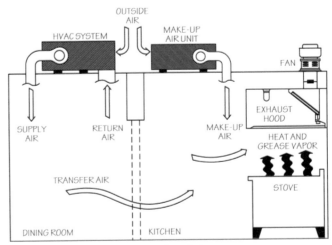

Various examples of air movement

All buildings have to deal with some regulations governing ventilation; air quality, air movement, and so on. The restaurant industry is often singled out to meet specific, and frequently, more stringent air quality standards. The focus on "sick-building syndrome," endeavoring to create clean, odor-free and smoke-free environments, is providing an increased public awareness.

Exhaust Air

Exhaust air is the starting point in restaurant kitchen ventilation. Exhaust air is the air contaminated by smoke and grease-laden vapors (aerosols), created from cooking sources. Without exhaust systems, kitchens would not only be in serious violation of building and fire codes, but kitchen employees and dining patrons could experience eye and nasal irritation, along with other health risks.

The volume of air to be removed (measured in cubic feet, or meters, per minute is referred to as "CFM"/"CMM") depends on the type of exhaust system and a host of other factors, such as:

- Design of hood(s)

- Fuel source(s)

- Presence of combustion products (and by-products)

- Type of cooking equipment

- Types/style of cooking

- Air currents present from (other) heat sources

- Allowable exhaust air temperatures

- Filter Type

- Type and location of makeup air

- Barriers to air circulation, such as walls and enclosures

- Disrupting air currents from registers, doorways and pass-through openings

A test hood with cooking line and smoke generator displaying how the exhaust system works. Courtesy of Greenheck.

Air velocities and volumes are referred to at NFPA 96, Section 8.2:

- Velocities in ducts shall not be less than 365.8 m/min (1200 ft/min) when operating. A duct velocity of 548.6 m/min (1800 ft/min) is typical when operating, 152.4 m/min (500 ft/min) in idle mode.

- Transitional ducts connecting the hood to ducts or ducts to fans need not maintain this velocity

- Air volumes for hoods shall be sufficient to provide for capture and remove all cooking vapors

- With the use of a variable speed device to control fan speed, in-duct velocity air speed during no-load cooking times may be reduced to a minimum of 152.4 m/min (500 ft/min)

- Test data, performance requirements must be available on request

Makeup Air

Makeup or compensating air must be supplied to replace kitchen air that has been exhausted. Makeup air should come from outside. This can be accomplished by including a makeup component within the HVAC system or by installing a makeup unit, either directly linked to or separate from the kitchen exhaust system.

Blowers (fans) specifically for such use typically introduce makeup air directly around the vicinity of the hood. Depending on the climate, tempering (heating or cooling) of makeup air is a common practice.

> *NFPA 96, Section 8.3.1: Replacement air quantity shall be adequate to prevent negative pressures in the commercial cooking area(s) from exceeding 4.98 Pa (0.02 in. water column).*

Front face canopy makeup air hood

Air for Combustion and Ventilation

All appliances that burn fuel need air for combustion and ventilation. Usually, a lack of air is not an issue for kitchen appliances, although makeup air is a requirement for exhaust systems.

Mechanical design engineers attempt to create a lower pressure zone in the kitchen. Air will naturally move from a higher pressure area (dining room) to a lower pressure area (kitchen). Cooking odors are thereby prevented from entering the dining (and other) areas.

Exhaust Flow Rates

In the past, the exhaust flow rate mandated by NFPA 96 was a range between 457.2 m/min (1500 ft/min) to 762 m/min (2500 ft/min). Most industry designers used a nominal rate of 548.6 m/min (1800 ft/min).

That changed when NFPA 96 recognized a new lower threshold of 152.4 m/min (500 ft/min). The ICC's International Mechanical Code has followed and also recognizes this lower range as acceptable.

The change came about for multiple reasons. First, the industry began the process of using variable speed fan technology. This technology is widely used in other areas of a building, but never before in conjunction with CKV hoods.

The problem is that most CKV exhaust fan systems in use today operate at a single speed. In other words, they are always running at full speed even when cooking equipment sits idle.

Variable speed fan testing has proved unequivocally that significant amounts of energy are wasted day after day by foodservice operations. Multiple test sites indicated that when existing operations were retrofitted and monitored, energy consumption was cut by amounts as much as 50% and more. That includes normal periods of heavy duty cooking. In the large majority of cases, the fan never operates again at the full design load after introduction of the variable speed technology.[1]

The second major concern involves grease deposits on the inside surfaces of Type I ductwork. After ASHRAE commissioned the University of Minnesota to develop a test method, it was conclusively proved that lower fan speed and therefore slower movement of the grease laden air did not increase deposition inside the ductwork. When those test results were released, first NFPA and later the ICC agreed to accept the conclusions and accept 152.4 m/min (500 ft/min) as the lower threshold of air speed.

Note: This does not mean that designers are or should be designing new installations to 152.4 m/min (500 ft/min). The 548.6 m/min (1800 ft/min) standard is still recognized as the nominal speed.

A second benefit is realized in existing building situations. Traditionally there was no previous ability to expand cooking operations by adding additional equipment and hood(s). In order to expand, it would normally require a new duct and shaft. Many older or high-rise buildings could not support adding additional cooking loads due to the fixed size of the duct. The nature of multiple floor buildings makes it almost impossible to add a new shaft through a varying mix of rooms and spaces on each floor.

Since Type I kitchen exhaust ducts must be enclosed in a fire rated protective enclosure or shaft up to the roof, it was impossible to add CFM capacity without increasing fan speed to an unacceptable level in the past.

The new lower exhaust flow rate means that these situations can be reviewed in light of this newer information and the change in codes. The University of Minnesota testing has shown that operating at a lower velocity than 548.6 m/min (1800 ft/min) can be accomplished successfully and safely.

Test and Balancing

Also referred to as system integration, testing and balancing is required to bring all the system components into a smooth functioning and effective CKV system.[2]

In new installations, it is common for the HVAC contractor to measure and adjust the results of his work.

It has been discovered that in many CKV systems that are performing poorly, it was questionable readings and calculations by the original installing contractor that caused the problem. For this reason, it is imperative that there be qualified third party testing and balancing.

---

[1] For a detailed report on the test completed at the San Francisco Mark Hopkins kitchen, go to http://www.fishnick.com.

[2] For a complete explanation, refer to ASHRAE's 2007 HANDBOOK, Chapter 31.

Note: To accurately test and balance the cooking equipment, it must be in operation (creating normal heat) to provide a necessary thermal plume. When the testing is done without the cooking appliances in place or not operating (cold) the readings will be incorrect resulting in poor exhaust performance.

Over time existing operations are subject to modifications by new appliances being added, changes in position and poor maintenance. The exhaust may be operating under very different conditions than when first designed or installed.

Architects should include third part testing in their bid specifications.

Proper test and balancing addresses the following:

- Measures and adjusts airflows in adjacent spaces or rooms

- Measures and adjusts airflows at each hood

- Corrects building pressures

- Corrects for hot/cold spots within adjacent spaces or rooms

- Tests motor voltage and amperages

- Adjusts fan speeds and belt tension

- Identifies greasy fans and motors

- Identifies cracked, worn or frayed belts

Exhaust System Configurations

A basic kitchen exhaust system consists of a hood, duct, and fan. For our purpose, an exhaust "system" is defined as one fan that may serve multiple hoods and ducts. Depending on the size of the cooking facility, there may be more than one system.

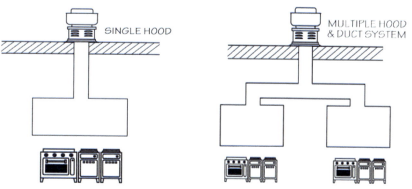

Appliances under one hood (under 3 meters or 12 feet) connected to a duct leading to a fan on the roof

Two hoods, each with one duct coming out of the top then joining a horizontal duct that takes a 90-degree turn and leads to a fan on the roof

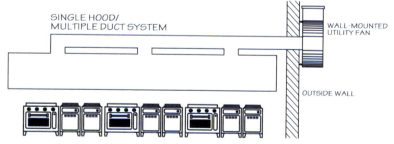

A long hood (over 3 m or 12 ft) with three ducts coming out of the top leading to a horizontal duct, that exits the side of the building at a wall mounted fan (or to the roof as shown in the first two illustrations)

Type I vs. Type II Exhaust Systems

Commercial kitchen exhaust systems are defined as either Type I or Type II. Type I exhaust systems are required over all grease producing appliances. Type I systems must be constructed, installed and maintained to meet the minimum requirements of the ICC and NFPA 96 Standard. These requirements deal primarily with fire safety and protection.

Type II systems are allowed <u>only</u> over non-grease producing applications such as heat, steam and odor removal.[3] These systems are <u>not</u> allowed over any grease producing appliance. Type II systems are not applicable to the NFPA 96 Standard.

Editorial Note: Throughout this manual we use the expression "Type I" to imply a system designed for grease exhaust applications which must meet minimum ICC and NFPA 96 requirements. The expression "Type II" refers to non-compliant systems over grease producing appliances and not approved for grease exhaust applications. There are a number of reasons an exhaust system would be considered non-compliant. Type II construction is only one of them.

General Construction Requirements

NFPA 96, 17A and ICC requirements are specific in the way these systems must be constructed and installed. As stated, the entire exhaust system must be able to withstand fire. These fire safety requirements mean that the exhaust system is much more than just an air moving system. Large amounts of time and money have gone into testing and researching the best ways to construct and install these systems to ensure maximum fire safety.

> *NFPA 96, Section 4.1.1: Cooking equipment used in processes producing smoke or grease-laden vapors shall be equipped with an exhaust system that complies with all the equipment and performance requirements of this standard.*
>
> *4.1.1.1* Cooking equipment that has been listed in accordance with ANSI/UL 197 or an equivalent standard for reduced emissions shall not be required to be provided with an exhaust system.*

Additional NFPA 96, Section 4.1 statements:

- All appliances and exhaust components must be kept in good working condition

- The system owner is ultimately responsible for the inspection, maintenance and cleanliness of the ventilation and fire protection equipment, unless the responsibility has been transferred in writing, to a management company, tenant, or other party.

- All interior surfaces of the exhaust system shall be accessible for cleaning and inspection purposes

- Drawings of the exhaust system installation as well as operating instructions for subassemblies and components and electrical schematics shall be kept on the premise[4]

- The Authority Having Jurisdiction (AHJ) may require written notification of any alteration, replacement, or relocation of any appliances or components of the exhaust or extinguishing system

---

[3] See NFPA 96, Section A.3.3.34.

[4] See NFPA 96, Sections 4.6 and 4.7.

Fire

Grease fires can reach temperatures of 1260ºC (2300ºF). The CKV system should be designed and constructed to draw fire in and away from vulnerable areas (such as other kitchen appliances and combustible materials). The system must be able to contain a small flare-up or a short term fire on the cooking appliances.

Theoretically, a commercial kitchen exhaust system should be able to contain larger, out-of-control fires, even if the fire-extinguishing system fails. Fire is drawn up into the hood and duct by the fan and buoyant force of the flame plume. Clearances and enclosures around the duct must prevent the fire from escaping into combustible concealed spaces. The duct termination must prevent the ignition of roof materials and not allow fire to enter building openings, such as HVAC, windows or doors.

The above "theory" <u>assumes</u> that the exhaust system is not heavily contaminated with grease. The exhaust system must extract and drain the maximum amount of grease in order to limit the amount of fuel. This grease extraction (cleaning) requires regular maintenance by kitchen staff and/or outside contractors. Eliminating grease buildup (fuel) will increase the probability that a fire can be controlled by a properly installed and maintained exhaust system.

Note: The fire-extinguishing system in the hood and duct should be considered as extinguishing devices <u>not</u> containment devices. Containment is the responsibility of the exhaust system.

Clearances

The intense heat from a duct fire can radiate out, igniting nearby combustibles (building structures or stored materials). Therefore, clearances to combustibles are unquestionably one of the most serious issues relating to fires in exhaust systems. Any combustible material in close proximity can be a factor in the propagation of fire beyond the exhaust system.

> *NFPA 96, Section 4.2.1 Where enclosures are not required, hoods, grease removal devices, exhaust fans, and ducts shall have a clearance of at least 457 mm (18 in.) to combustible material, 76 mm (3 in.) to limited-combustible material, and 0 mm (0 in.) to noncombustible material.*

These clearance requirements apply to more than just building materials. They also include the need to keep storage products and other combustible objects away from the hood and duct (such as boxes of paper products, packaged foods and other items).

For more discussion on Clearances and Reduction Methods, see Chapter 6, Ducts and Fans.

Radiant heat from a fire burned through the drywall

The casing around this duct saved the building from total destruction

Fire Containment

Vent and Control

Vent and Control (the main premise of NFPA 96) means that the fire is purposefully drawn away from vulnerable areas (such as a combustible ceiling) and allowed to burn in the properly constructed and installed environment of the exhaust system. The fire is confined in the duct and "drowned" by air (oxygen) from the fan.

For example, when there is a fire on the appliances, the fan is left running, pulling the fire into the exhaust system where it can extinguish itself.

Fire is a good servant but a poor master

Compartmentalize and Sacrifice

Another approach is to contain a fire in a controllable space or area. There may be a need to purposely sacrifice a section or "unit" - but it is done to save the rest of the building. A kitchen exhaust system that is on fire may be sealed off by the use of dampers built into the hood assembly and the fire left to burn only within the hood, thereby preventing fire from entering the duct. Fire fighters that battle blazes in apartment blocks will often use this approach. A decision is made to seal off one apartment and then to concentrate fire-fighting efforts around the outer perimeter of this burning unit.

Restaurant going up in smoke

Contain and Control

For lack of a better definition, Contain and Control is a cross between the previous two approaches. Efforts are made to contain the fire in a manageable space - not to vent it, but also not to sacrifice the unit or area. Listed water wash hoods are essentially designed on this principle. Fire-extinguishing equipment is built into the hood and is the first line of defense. If the extinguisher fails, dampers close and the water system activates. The dampers are also intended to compartmentalize the fire in the kitchen area. For more on the function of "fire protection" by water wash hoods, see Chapter 4, Hoods.

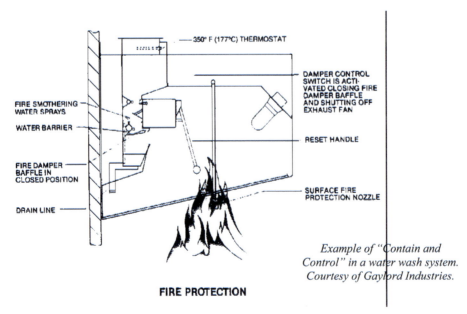

FIRE SMOTHERING WATER SPRAYS

WATER BARRIER

FIRE DAMPER BAFFLE IN CLOSED POSITION

DRAIN LINE

350° F (177°C) THERMOSTAT

DAMPER CONTROL SWITCH IS ACTIVATED CLOSING FIRE DAMPER BAFFLE AND SHUTTING OFF EXHAUST FAN

RESET HANDLE

SURFACE FIRE PROTECTION NOZZLE

FIRE PROTECTION

Example of "Contain and Control" in a water wash system. Courtesy of Gaylord Industries.

Chapter Two - Codes and Responsibilities

CODES AND RESPONSIBILITIES...2

   Codes and Standards...2

   Codes and Standards Organizations...2

      National Fire Protection Association 2

      NFPA Code and Standard Definitions..3

      Equipment Approval and Listing Definitions 4

      NFPA 96 4

   International Code Council 6

      International Mechanical Code 6

      ICC versus NFPA 96 6

   Listing Agencies...7

      Other Resource Bodies 7

      Installation Challenges...8

   System Installation and Performance Evaluation 8

   Trade Responsibilities...8

      General Areas of Responsibility 8

   Key Changes to the NFPA 96 Standard 11

      NFPA Sections...11

This was a real situation! Someone's creation of a "hood" for their toaster oven.

Codes and Responsibilities

Codes and Standards

The construction of buildings is regulated by building codes and supported by standards. Codes define various occupancy characteristics of buildings and establish basic construction features and performance criteria. Standards establish acceptable practices for meeting the minimum criteria and are generally referenced by the codes.

Codes and standards are continually evolving. They lag technology; as they have typically been written after incidents have occurred, research results are available, and new products have been developed and proven. Additionally, their process of development and adoption can take years. It is common in most jurisdictions that existing buildings are governed by the codes and standards that were adopted at the time of construction. Cooking equipment, exhaust systems, and fire-extinguishing systems are governed by codes and standards in effect at the time of their installation. Conversely, facility operational aspects, fire safety practices, and system maintenance practices are governed by current fire prevention codes and referenced system standards.

George Zawacki and Phil speaking at an NFPA convention in Las Vegas

It is a never-ending task to keep abreast of applicable codes, but a thorough knowledge of them is critical to understand the background of a commercial cooking facility.

In addition to codes and standards, system design, installation, and maintenance requirements of equipment manufacturers must be followed. These requirements are typically part of the terms of product and system listings by UL or other third party testing agencies.

Codes and Standards Organizations

In the U.S. and Canada, state/provincial and local jurisdictions usually adopt a model code with supporting standards. Some jurisdictions make substantial amendments or prepare their own building and fire codes. Once adopted, the code becomes an enforceable legal document administered by various authorities within the jurisdiction. The requirements for commercial cooking facilities are addressed in the building, fire prevention, mechanical, fuel gas, electrical, and life safety codes.

Model codes and standards are developed by various private sector independent standards development organizations. There are presently two major code development organizations in the US and Canada in reference to commercial kitchens, which offer model codes for state/provincial and local adoption. They are:

- The National Fire Protection Association – NFPA
- The International Code Council – ICC

These bodies are made up of expert volunteers from industry, government, building and fire officials, as well as professionals from engineering, insurance and other interests. The technical committees of these organizations meet at regular intervals and review changing technologies, construction and other innovations that may affect the building trade or fire safety needs of the community. When dealing with suggested code changes these various bodies have differing procedures and protocols with varying degrees of involvement among interested parties. But all have the primary focus of improving fire safety.

National Fire Protection Association

National Fire Protection Association (NFPA) codes and standards are developed through a consensus process approved by ANSI. The process brings together volunteers representing varied viewpoints and interests to achieve balanced consensus on fire and other safety issues.

The NFPA administers the process and establishes rules, within the American National Standards Institute (ANSI) criteria, to promote fairness in the consensus development system. It also seeks research support through such organizations as the Fire Protection Research Foundation and the National Institute of Standards and Technology (NIST) to validate existing and new code requirements.[1]

Further, NFPA partners with other code development organizations such as:

- The International Association of Plumbing and Mechanical Officials (IAPMO) who develop the Uniform Mechanical Code

- The Western Fire Chiefs (WFC) to develop the NFPA 1 Uniform Fire Code

Codes relevant to commercial cooking equipment and exhaust systems are:

- NFPA 5000 Building Construction and Safety Code

- NFPA 1 Uniform Fire Code

- NFPA 70 National Electrical Code

- NFPA 54 National Fuel Gas Code

- NFPA 72 National Fire Alarm Code

- NFPA 101 Life Safety Code

Some of the NFPA standards that relate to specific kitchen components are:

- NFPA 10 Standard for Portable Extinguishers

- NFPA 17 Standard for Dry Chemical Extinguishing Systems

- NFPA 17A Standard for Wet Chemical Extinguishing Systems

- NFPA 96 Standard for Ventilation Control and Fire Protection of Commercial Cooking Operations

NFPA Code and Standard Definitions

Code – A standard that is an extensive compilation of provisions covering broad subject matter or that is suitable for adoption into law independently of other codes and standards.[2]

Standard – A document, the main text of which contains only mandatory provisions using the word "shall" to indicate requirements and which is in form generally suitable for mandatory reference by another standard or code or for adoption into law. Nonmandatory provisions shall be located in an appendix or annex, footnote, or fine-print note and are not to be considered a part of the requirements of a standard.

Note: The decision whether to designate a standard as a "code" is based on such factors as the size and scope of the document, its intended use and form of adoption, and whether it contains substantial enforcement and administrative provisions.

Recommended Practice – A document similar in content and structure to a code or standard but that contains only nonmandatory provisions using the word "should" to indicate recommendations in the body of the text.

Guide – A document that is advisory or informative in nature and that contains only nonmandatory provisions. A guide may contain mandatory statements such as when a guide can be used, but the document as a whole is not suitable for adoption into law.

Shall – Indicates a mandatory requirement.

Should – Indicates a recommendation or that which is advised but not required.

---

[1] *For more information about NFPA codes and standards and the NFPA standards procedure go to NFPA's web site at www.nfpa.org; select "Codes & Standards."*

[2] *Terms are as per the NFPA Glossary of Terms. This is available online at http://www.nfpa.org/assets/files/PDF/definitions.pdf.*

Equipment Approval and Listing Definitions

Approved – Acceptable to the authority having jurisdiction.

Note: The National Fire Protection Association does not approve, inspect, or certify any installations, procedures, equipment, or materials nor does it approve or evaluate testing laboratories. In determining the acceptability of installations or procedures, equipment, or materials, the "authority having jurisdiction" may base acceptance on compliance with NFPA or other appropriate standards. In the absence of such standards said authority may require evidence of proper installation, procedure, or use. The "authority having jurisdiction" may also refer to the listings or labeling practices of an organization that is concerned with product evaluation and is thus in a position to determine compliance with appropriate standards for the current production of listed items.

> *Listed – Equipment, materials, or services included in a list published by an organization that is acceptable to the authority having jurisdiction and concerned with evaluation of products or services, that maintains periodic inspection of production of listed equipment or materials or periodic evaluation of services, and whose listing states that either the equipment, material, or service meets appropriate designated standards or has been tested and found suitable for specified purpose.*

Note: The means for identifying listed equipment may vary for each organization concerned with product evaluation; some organizations do not recognize equipment as listed unless it is also labeled. The authority having jurisdiction should utilize the system employed by the listing organization to identify a listed product.

NFPA 96

The NFPA *Technical Committee on Venting Systems for Cooking Appliances*, organized by the NFPA Standards Council in 1987, is responsible for NFPA 96. The NFPA 96 Committee is an evolution from the NFPA 91 Blower and Exhaust Committee, which first published requirements on the subject of cooking equipment ventilation subject in 1946. This subject was later the responsibility of the Chimneys and Heating Equipment Committee. This committee first developed the NFPA 96 standard in 1961.

NFPA 96 sets forth requirements for the design, construction and installation of commercial kitchen systems.

For ongoing maintenance and operations, NFPA 96 is regarded (in most areas) as the governing standard, and it is referenced by model building and fire codes, as well as state and local codes. Codes governing facility operations are generally retroactive, whereas codes governing construction are generally not.

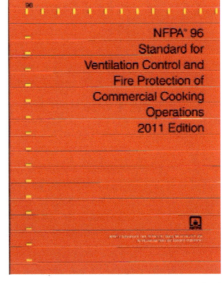

NFPA® 96
Standard for
Ventilation Control and
Fire Protection of
Commercial Cooking
Operations
2011 Edition

Since its inception, the document has matured to include specific construction requirements for both ventilation and fire protection equipment needed for the safe operation of commercial cooking equipment. In recent years, requirements for re-circulating systems, duct wrap, clearances to combustibles, and enclosure requirements have been added. In the 1998 edition the inclusion of a specific "Ventilation Inspection" requirement added the protocol of having the ductwork regularly inspected. In 2001 an extensive rewrite of NFPA 96 resulted in new numbering for most sections.

NFPA 96 Administrative Requirements

The authority having jurisdiction must work within a framework of laws and regulations. To assist the AHJ, the NFPA 96 Standard lays out a relatively specific Scope and Purpose for where the standard can be applied.

> *NFPA 96, Section 1.1.1*: This standard shall provide the minimum fire safety requirements (preventative and operative) related to the design, installation, operation, inspection, and maintenance of all public and private cooking operations.*

> *1.1.2 This standard shall apply to residential cooking equipment used for commercial cooking operations.*

1.1.3 This standard shall not apply to cooking equipment located in a single dwelling unit.

1.1.4* This standard shall not apply to facilities where all of the following are met:

(1) Only residential equipment is being used.

(2) Fire Extinguishers located in all kitchen areas in accordance with NFPA 10, Standard for Portable Fire Extinguishers.

(3) Facility is not an assembly occupancy.

(4) Subject to the approval of the authority having jurisdiction.

1.2 Purpose. The purpose of this standard shall be to reduce the potential fire hazard of cooking operations, irrespective of the type of cooking equipment used and whether used in public or private facilities.

The application of the NFPA 96 Standard by the authority having jurisdiction.

NFPA 96, Section 1.3 Application.

1.3.1* This standard shall be applied as a united whole.

A.1.3.1 This standard cannot provide safe design and operation if parts of it are not enforced or are arbitrarily deleted in any application.

1.3.2 The authority having jurisdiction shall determine compliance with this standard and authorize equivalent deviations from it in all applications.

The Standard also takes into consideration the need for the AHJ to make judgment calls where new technology, experience and better understanding of potential fire hazards have been found.

NFPA 96, Section 1.4 Retroactivity. The provisions of this standard reflect a consensus of what is necessary to provide an acceptable degree of protection from the hazards addressed in this standard at the time the standard was issued.

1.4.1 Unless otherwise specified, the provisions of this standard shall not apply to facilities, equipment, structures, or installations that existed or were approved for construction or installation prior to the effective date of the standard. Where specified, the provisions of this standard shall be retroactive.

1.4.2 In those cases where the authority having jurisdiction determines that the existing situation presents an unacceptable degree of risk, the authority having jurisdiction shall be permitted to apply retroactively any portions of this standard.

1.4.3 The retroactive requirements of this standard shall be permitted to be modified if their application clearly would be impractical in the judgment of the authority having jurisdiction, and only where it is clearly evident that a reasonable degree of safety is provided.

1.5 Equivalency. Nothing in this standard is intended to prevent the use of systems, methods, or devices of equivalent or superior quality, strength, fire resistance, effectiveness, durability, and safety over those prescribed by this standard.

1.5.1 Technical documentation shall be submitted to the authority having jurisdiction to demonstrate equivalency.

1.5.2 The system, method, or device shall be approved for the intended purpose by the authority having jurisdiction.

These standards provide the AHJ with the power to improve potentially unsafe situations within the exhaust or fire-extinguishing systems. These sections have been most notably used to upgrade fire-extinguishing systems to the new UL 300 standard and to improve accessibility in the exhaust system for grease removal by requiring hinge kits on fans and access panels; both of which are only recent developments.

International Code Council

Historically there were three primary model building code writing organizations in the U.S. These included:[3]

- BOCA – Building Officials and Code Administration International

- ICBO – International Conference of Building Officials

- SBCCI – Southern Building Code Congress International

These organizations produced model building, mechanical, fuel gas, and fire prevention codes.

In 1994, the International Code Council (ICC) was organized with the purpose of lessening the burdens of regulation through the development and publication of a single set of national model construction codes for adoption and use by state and local government. The ICC is an umbrella organization of the BOCA, ICBO and SBCCI parent organizations.

Interested individuals and groups submit proposed code changes to ICC documents. A committee of code regulators and construction industry representatives consider the proposed changes. Code change hearings are held, and each of the above three model code groups review the changes and vote to determine the final action.

Codes developed by the ICC include the:

- International Building Code
- Electrical Administrative Provisions
- International Fuel Gas Code

- International Mechanical Code
- International Plumbing Code
- International Fire Code

International Mechanical Code

The International Mechanical Code (IMC), developed by ICC, is one of the two primary Codes/Standards used for the design, construction and installation of commercial kitchen systems. It is considered a comprehensive mechanical code, which establishes minimum requirements for mechanical systems using prescriptive and performance-related provisions.

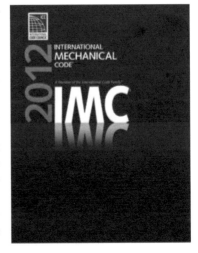

In 1997, many jurisdictions accepted the International Mechanical Code as the model code for commercial kitchen exhaust systems. Chapter 5, Sections 506-507 covers construction of commercial kitchen exhaust systems and corresponding building components; Section 508 covers commercial kitchen makeup air systems, and Section 509 contains requirements for fire-extinguishing systems.

IMC does not presently cover maintenance requirements of exhaust or fire-extinguishing systems; however it references the International Fire Code, which does.

ICC versus NFPA 96

Throughout state and local jurisdictions in the United States and Canada the provision of building and fire codes differ. Building codes, enforced by building officials, govern the construction of a building and may reference ICC for the design and construction of a kitchen exhaust system or the requirements of other fire safety coverage's of specific appliances. However, after completion of the building, a fire prevention code, enforced by fire officials, may be the governing code, and it may reference NFPA 96. Although these two documents are similar, there are differences in the degree of guidance the various components provide.[4] Additionally, many jurisdictions create their own Building or Fire Codes.

---

[3] *For more information about ICC codes and the ICC code process go to the ICC web site, www.iccsafe.org.*

[4] *For a comprehensive comparison between the NFPA and IMC go to http://www.philackland.com/docs/Comparative_Matrix_1st_Edition.pdf*

Listing Agencies

There are a number of testing laboratories, which test and list the various products and systems. Some of the most familiar are:

- Underwriters Laboratories Inc.
- Underwriters Laboratories of Canada
- FM Global
- Canadian Safety Association
- Inchcape/ ETL
- Omega Point

These agencies work with equipment manufacturers to test products before they are brought to market, thereby protecting society from faulty or flawed designs. They are also recognized by code and standard development organizations, which use the product and system test findings when considering new requirements.

When a product (and in some cases, system) has been evaluated, it is placed on a "List" of products that have passed a particular product standard. This is what being "Listed" means. Any product that is listed will have the label of the listing organization applied on it. This label will provide information on the listing, such as manufacturer's name, product category, etc. Specific information may accompany listed products regarding their installation, use and maintenance.

Grease filters, exhaust (including water wash) hoods, hood lighting fixtures, grease ducts, exhaust fans, and fire-extinguishing systems are listed. Many other components are also listed such as access panels, duct wrap, and hood and duct accessories.

In most jurisdictions, anything that is appropriately "Listed" (or Classified) is acceptable to the Authority Having Jurisdiction (AHJ). The challenge for an inspector is to confirm that the product is actually listed for <u>commercial kitchen use</u>. Up-blast fans are a classic case in point. Contractors (and manufacturers) may claim a fan is "listed" because it has some component that is listed (like the electric motor, switch or some other component). But the <u>entire fan</u> is required to be listed "for commercial kitchen use". There should be a label identifying it as listed.

NFPA 96 clearly defines "listed" to mean listed for that specified purpose. Therefore a listed upblast fan must be specifically listed for use in a commercial cooking application.[5]

Note: On some products, such as listed hoods, a listing label may not appear on every single component. Components like doors and panels or control cabinets will not carry the label, but are part of the listed product. The inspector should confirm a component's listing with the manufacturer.

Other Resource Bodies

There are a number of professionally recognized associations that provide guidance. For example:

- Air Movement and Control Association International, Inc (AMCA)
- American Society of Heating, Refrigerating and Air Conditioning Engineers (ASHRAE)
- NSF International (formerly National Sanitation Foundation)

---

[5] *See NFPA 96, Section 8.1.1.1.*

Installation Challenges

In a large number of cases, exhaust and fire-extinguishing technicians are not brought into the design process early enough. The usual scenario is that the building is completed before kitchen exhaust and fire-extinguishing systems are considered, or the exhaust/fire-extinguishing systems are a "tenant improvement" in an existing building. In either case, compromises to fire safety may take place.

Additionally, the mechanical engineer, framer, and the hood installer should know each other's requirements. Inspectors need to scrutinize the plans and the under-construction building at a number of stages, such as design, pre-framing, pre-interior finish, and preoperational to consider the interrelationship requirements of fire prevention and extinguishing. Rated shafts (which enclose the exhaust duct) are one of the most important issues that need to be addressed early in the process. Additionally, dimensions, fire resistance rating, and ceilings all require consideration during the construction phase. It is difficult to apply fire-safe interior framing if the kitchen layout has not been designed and approved in advance. This lack of continuity creates situations that contribute to fires.

System Installation and Performance Evaluation

When evaluating system installation and performance, establish a chain of responsibility for the exhaust and fire-extinguishing systems. This will require the review of installation permits and contracts. In addition to establishing the specific editions of codes and standards in effect, the system analysis will also require the review of information such as drawings, testing laboratory listing requirements and manufacturer's system installation instructions.

Many existing CKV systems do not meet current codes and standards, posing fire development or spread hazards, as well as life safety concerns, especially if the kitchen is part of an assembly occupancy.

Trade Responsibilities

Building Inspectors must assess the responsibilities and requirements of designing and installing a commercial kitchen ventilation system.

At the design phase it is imperative that both intake and exhaust air are calculated, or air balancing and a host of other air movement difficulties are created.

General Areas of Responsibility

Architects

The following lists are only general and basic outlines.

Areas in which Architects need to provide information to the AHJ:

- Type of occupancy of its individual spaces

- Special conditions of fire protection design

- Overall function of the structure

- Fire-resistive walls, floor-ceiling assemblies, roof-ceiling assemblies

- Protection of openings

- Horizontal and vertical smoke barriers

- Appropriate fire separations

Design Plans should show the following:

- Necessary horizontal and vertical fire separations

- The hourly requirements of the fire separation

- Clearance-to-combustible requirements on the floor plans and in building sections

- Listed fire-resistive assemblies must be identified by their design number or specification as well as by hourly rates. The kitchen ventilation system designer can then determine the maximum ceiling opening permitted in the assembly and the type of opening protection required.

- HVAC air intake direction

- Rooftop unit locations

- Proposed exhaust locations

- Interior ceiling construction

- Location of windows and doors near kitchen exhaust termination point

- Location and type of all wall assemblies and fire separations

- Location of plumbing (floor drains)

- Noise level compliance

The architect should specify that the wall, ceiling and floor systems contractor(s) provide access openings in building structures that are of a size and location adequate for safe access to fire dampers, access panels and other equipment by maintenance personnel.

Engineers/System Designers

To confirm accountability, require designers to provide all the necessary documentation in the initial design phase. Many times the exhaust system is designed by one of the major component manufacturers, such as the water wash hood manufacturer. Their primary focus may only be insuring that their component is installed in the system. This may create a situation where other components are not given the same level of consideration. This, in turn, could cause a system to be difficult or impossible to balance, or other areas (primarily duct installation) to not receive the same level of scrutiny.

Use of standard symbols for the method is highly recommended.

Fire Inspector checking hood and suppression system

Building Inspectors should verify acceptance of the methods and equipment to be used before approval of any plans.

Building and mechanical plans and drawings need to show the following specifications:

- Location of ducts, pipes and other conduits, pierce-requiring fire-rated separations or smoke barriers

- Fire and smoke dampers and heat stops

- The hourly rating and type of damper and requirements of access doors

- Specific framing requirements of openings

- Duct penetrations requiring protection

- Location of emergency exits in relation to the kitchen exhaust system(s)

- Adequate support for mechanical units (air pollution control units, fans, heat recovery units)

- Makeup air requirements

- Barrier locations

- Occupancy assignments

- Protection planning

- Rating and identification of compartments

- Structural components

- The location and mounting details of all automatic fire doors, dampers, access panels, and other fire protection equipment incorporated in the exhaust and makeup systems

Note: Means by which thickness and types of fire resistive materials are rated may vary with the jurisdiction.

Contractors/Installers

The contractor or installer should have a working knowledge of the components they are installing, including subassemblies, such as:

- Fire and/or smoke dampers

- Access openings/panels

- Ceiling opening protections

- Dampers

- Access panels

- Heat stops

- Tippable fans in locations specified by the plans

Inspector's class on Vancouver Island, BC, Canada

- Adequate wiring for exhaust fan shut off on roof

- Grease interceptor size and location

- Installation of all fire-extinguishing system pull stations, alarms, detectors, emergency lights, exit signs, and exit directional signs

- Fire alarms

- Fuel shut off

- Makeup air interlocks

- Clearance to combustibles

All installations need to be accessible for servicing, cleaning and inspection.

For further information on the responsibilities of sheet metal contractors, see the *SMACNA Kitchen Ventilation Systems and Food Service Equipment Fabrication & Installation Guidelines.*

Key Changes to the NFPA 96 Standard

The following are some of the key changes to the NFPA 96 Standard from the 2008 to the 2011 Edition.[6]

NFPA Sections

Definitions

3.3.37 Maintenance. Work, including, but not limited to, repair, replacement, and service, performed to ensure that equipment operates properly.

3.3.39 Non-Compliant. Not meeting all applicable requirements of this standard.

This wording provides conformity and clarification to the standard

General Requirements

4.1.5 The responsibility for inspection, testing, maintenance, and cleanliness of the ventilation control and fire protection of the commercial cooking operation shall ultimately be that of the owner of the system provided that this responsibility has not been transferred in written form to a management company, tenant or other party.

The change from the 2008 is only an editorial correction, but it is an important standard when clarifying responsibilties.

Hoods

5.5.1 Duct systems connected to Ultraviolet Hoods shall comply with Chapter 7 (Ducts).

There have been several installations where the ductwork has been light-weight steel instead of that called for by the NFPA 96 Standard. This is putting too much reliance on the ability of the UV and maintenance staff to keep the UV system running properly.

Filter Protection -- Baffle Plate

6.2.2.3 The baffle plate shall be sized and located so that flames or combustion gases shall travel a distance not less than 457.2 mm (18 in.) from the heat source to the grease removal device.

6.2.2.4 The baffle shall be located not less than 6 in. (152.4 mm) from the grease removal devices.

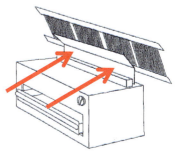

This illustration was added to the Standard to assist inspectors recognize the need for protection of the filters from heat.

Example of a baffle placed on the edge of the flue gas exhaust that will deflect heat and flames from the filters.

NFPA 96 2011 Fig. A.6.2.2.2

Exhaust Ducts

7.4.2.3 If not easily accessible from the floor or a 3 m (10 ft) stepladder, openings on vertical grease ducts shall be provided with safe access and a work platform.

Safe access must be provided to ensure the cleaning takes place. This language is similar to that for horizontal duct openings. For further details see Duct Openings in Chapter 6, Ducts and Fans.

---

[6] *Editorial Note:* ~~Strikethroughs~~ *indicate deletions and* <u>underlines</u> *additions to the final document. These are not all the changes; but are the ones we feel will have the greatest interest to the fire inspector.*

Auxiliary Equipment

9.3.1.3 Equipment shall have a space provided to all access panels or doors for the safe removal and servicing of control devices, such as filters, electrostatic precipitator cells, and odor control media beds, and for cleaning of the equipment housing.

It is pretty obvious that without access and space around the system to open and get into the equipment, maintenance will suffer. Yet, in many cases, other equipment, plumbing, wiring and what not is installed in such a way as to block access. This standard may help, but not likely. Inspectors need to be on the look out for blocked access or opening. For further details see Fire Doors in Chapter 6, Ducts and Fans.

Fire-Extinguishing

10.5.7 Instructions shall be provided to employees regarding the proper use of portable fire extinguishers and of the manual activation of fire-extinguishing equipment.

Training is necessary in both the use of the portables but more importantly in the activation of the fixed fire suppression system. Beyond getting extinguishing agent on the appliance fire, activating the fixed system will shut the gas off to the appliances. For further details see Staff Training in Chapter 5, Fire Extinguishing Systems.

Procedures for the Use Chapter 11 of the 2011 NFPA 96

Operating Procedures

11.1.6 Cooking equipment shall not be operated while its fire-extinguishing system or exhaust system is nonoperational or ~~otherwise~~ impaired.

"Red-Tagging"

11.1.6.1 Where the fire-extinguishing system or exhaust system is nonoperational or impaired, the systems shall be tagged noncompliant, and the owners or the owner's representative shall be notified in writing of the impairment.

This is one of the more controversial additions to the standard. Members had differencing views of the value of the addition. On the one side, it was said that this is a great 'sales tool' for service providers, as they could "run to mother" every time there is some need for improvement or adjustment of the suppression system. On the other hand, if they notified the AHJ, it could potentially force owners to fix serious problems that they might otherwise be inclined to ignore (until there is a fire).

Across North America, the practice of "red-tagging" suppression systems and what that actually means is very inconsistent. This issue should be one of considerable importance to the fire inspector. What is the policy in your department? For further details see Service Requirements in Chapter 7, Service Providers.

Replacing Certain Types of Suppression Heat Sensors

11.2.7 Fixed temperature-sensing elements other than the fusible metal alloy type shall be permitted to remain continuously in service, provided they are inspected and cleaned or replaced if necessary in accordance with the manufacturer's instruction, every 12 months or more frequently to ensure proper operation of the system.

This reflects the wording in the NFPA 17A. For further details see Automatic Water Sprinklers in Chapter 5, Fire Extinguishing Systems.

Grease Accumulation

11.4 Inspection of Grease Buildup. The entire exhaust system shall be inspected for grease buildup by a properly trained, qualified and certified ~~company or~~ person(s) acceptable to the authority having jurisdiction and in accordance with Table 11.4.

This new standard removes the word "company." The substantiation was, there needs to be a properly trained, qualified and certified (TQC) person doing the work. In many cases large companies are getting "certified" and then declaring that all their people are therefore "trained, qualified and certified" when they are not.[7]

---

[7] *Phil Ackland Certification (PAC) is very specific that there must be at least one certified individual on the cleaning or inspecting crew. If a cleaning company were to claim to be PAC and not have at least one individual on the job who is PAC, then their company qualification is void.*

What is your department's policy toward "licensing/recognizing" (holding responsible) any of these services required by commercial kitchen fire safety devices? For further details see Service Providers Chapter

Inspecting Listed Hoods

11.5 Inspection, <u>Testing</u> and Maintenance of Listed Hoods Containing Mechanical, Water Spray or Ultraviolet Devices.

Listed hoods containing mechanical or fire-actuated dampers, internal washing components, or other mechanically operated devices shall be inspected and tested by properly trained ~~and~~ qualified <u>and certified</u> persons every 6 months or at frequencies recommended by the manufacturer in accordance with their listings.

Although these changes are relatively minor, we have chosen to repeat 11.5 (from the 2008 edition) because of its major importance with overall fire safety. The reality is that a large number of listed hoods are not receiving mechanical maintenance. When inspectors encounter listed hoods containing any mechanical device, they should require the owner to provide proof of mechanical maintenance. For further details see Listed Exhaust Maintenance in Chapter 7, Service Providers.

11.6.1 Upon inspection, if exhaust system is found to be contaminated with deposits from grease-laden vapors, the contaminated portions of the exhaust system shall be cleaned by a properly trained, qualified, and certified ~~company or~~ person(s) acceptable to the authority having jurisdiction.

This change corresponds with the change to 11.4, removing the word "company." Ensuring that the individual in charge or the service will have the necessary knowledge. For further details see Kitchen Exhaust Cleaners in Chapter 7, Service Providers.

Solid Fuel

14.3.3 Exhaust systems serving solid fuel cooking equipment including gas or electrically operated equipment, shall be separate from all other exhaust systems.

14.3.4 Cooking processes, including but not limited to those that use any solid fuel for cooking enhancement or smoke flavoring, shall comply with 14.3.3. <u>and 14.8</u>.

14.8 Procedures for Inspection, Cleaning, and Maintenance for Solid Fuel Cooking. Solid fuel cooking appliances shall be inspected, cleaned, and maintained in accordance with procedures outlined in Chapter 11, and with 14.8.1 through 14.8.5.

The change was made to 14.3.4 (referencing 14.3.3 and 14.8) to ensure the inclusion of "smoke flavoring" to that of any other solid fuel application. There is an increasing trend to add pieces of hardwood, chips or other wood products near the gas fired burners of a charbroiler to enhance flavoring. What this does is introduce many of the negative elements of solid fuel (increased ash).

Where this practice is found, for fire safety, an inspector should consider the appliance as a solid fuel application and require corresponding safety factors.

14.7.6 Fire-extinguishing equipment shall be rated and designed to extinguish solid fuel cooking fires, ~~in accordance with the manufacturer's recommendations.~~

An inspector needs to ensure that the suppression methods used around solid fuel are adequate to extinguish a fire on the appliance and the surrounding area. The volume of an NFPA 17A type extinguisher may be limited and not adequate to control a large wood fire.

14.7.8* All solid fuel appliances (whether under a hood or not) with fire boxes of 0.14 m³ (5 ft³) volume or less shall have at least a listed 2-A rated water spray fire extinguisher or a 6 L (1.6 gal) wet chemical fire extinguisher listed for Class K fires in accordance with NFPA 10 <u>with a maximum travel distance of 6 m (20 feet) to the appliance.</u>

The distance to a portable may be critical in a solid fuel fire. Again, emphasis must be placed on activating the fixed suppression system first. For further details see Appliances Chapter – Solid Fuels. **The Proposed**

Editorial comments on 2014 Edition of NFPA 96 by Mark Conroy, Brooks Equipment

- The 2014 edition of the NFPA 96 will be published in the Fall of 2013. Below are a select number of points and comments by Mark Conroy of Brooks Equipment, who was present at the majority of the meetings of the 2013 revision cycle. The opinions are those of Mr. Conroy. [8]

Duct Enclosures

- A new paragraph 4.2.3.3 was added to allow a clearance reduction system of field-applied duct enclosure material, system, product, or method of construction listed to ASTM E 2336. (ROP 96-15)

Clearance to Limited Combustible Materials (Clarified)

- Paragraph 4.2.3.3 was clarified by making it into a list of items (a through e). It seems that it wasn't clear that "other combustible materials or assembly of noncombustible materials" and "materials and products that are listed for the purpose of reducing clearance" are completely separate items. The new list makes that clear. (ROC 96-8)

Grease Filters (NEW)

- Paragraph 6.2.3.1 was deleted and replaced with a sentence that requires grease filters to be listed. A new subparagraph requires those listed filters to be constructed of noncombustible material. (ROC 96-11)

Sloping of Ductwork (NEW)

- Paragraph 7.1.4 was replaced with 5 paragraphs and an annex explanation. The main paragraph will require ducts to be installed with a 2% slope for horizontal runs up to 75 ft. Over 75 ft, the slope needs to be 8%. The subparagraphs allow factory built ducts to be installed in accordance with their listing and manufacturer instructions, access in accordance with 7.4.1, drains at low points, and installed without dips and traps. The annex material explains that low points are difficult to avoid in runs over 75 ft and therefore drains are needed. (ROC 96-16)

Exhaust Duct Drains (NEW)

- A new provision was added as 7.1.4.3 to require drains that are provided in exhaust ducts to be either continuously welded to the exhaust duct or be listed. (ROP 96-32)

Access for Cleaning Near Wall Mounted Fans (NEW)

- A new paragraph 7.3.8 was added to require wall mounted fans to have access for cleaning within 3 ft of the exhaust fan. (ROP96-31)

Factory-Built Grease Ducts (NEW)

- A new paragraph 7.5.2.1.1 was added to allow factory-built grease ducts that are listed to ANSI/UL 1978 to incorporate non-welded joint construction in accordance with their listings. (ROP 96-33)

Grease Duct Leakage Test (NEW)

- A new leakage test requirement was added as 7.5.2.1.2 for grease duct systems to assure that the welded joints and seams are liquid tight. Also, new annex material explains that the test can be a light test or a water pressure test (through a pressure washer). (ROP 96-34)

Exhaust Fan Discharge (NEW)

- A third option was added to 7.8.2.1(9) to allow an exhaust fan discharge that is directed up and away from the roof surface. (ROP 96-41)

Exhaust Fan Listing Requirement (NEW)

- A new 8.1.1 was added to exhaust fans to be listed to UL 762. The existing paragraph 8.1.1 was modified slightly as a subparagraph, thereby meaning that upblast fans need to comply with this listing requirement. (ROP 96-42)

---

[8] • *Copyright material used with permission of Brooks Equipment Company, Charlotte, NC.*

Automatic Exhaust Fan Startup (NEW)

- A new requirement was added as 8.2.3.3 to mandate that exhaust fans be provided with a means so that the fan is activated when the appliance under the hood is turned on. (ROC 96-19)

Obsolete Fire Protection Systems (NEW)

- Paragraph 10.2.3.1 was modified to apply to all existing dry and wet chemical systems not in compliance with ANSI/UL 300. Additionally, a new paragraph 10.2.3.2 was added to mandate that all existing systems meet 10.2.3 by January 1, 2014. Regarding dry chemical systems protecting these hazards, they need to be taken out in accordance with the new 10.2.3.1 or 10.2.3.2 and replaced with systems complying with 10.2.3. (ROC96-22)

Water Mist Systems Added to List of Allowable Systems (NEW)

- Water mist systems complying with NFPA 750 was added to the list of systems permitted by 10.2.6. (ROP 96-52)

Sprinkler System Isolation Valves (NEW)

- A new requirement was added to 10.2.9 to mandate the installation of indicating control valves and drains so that the hood system and sprinkler systems can be controlled individually. (ROP 96-55)

Sprinkler System Hydraulic Calculations (NEW)

- A new 10.3.2.1 was added to require that hydraulic calculations consider both systems operating simultaneously where a sprinkler system is used in conjunction with a water-based system served by the same water supply. (ROP 96-56)

Portable Fire Extinguishers (Clarified)

- Clarifications were made to section 10.10 so that it matches NFPA 10. In essence, Class K extinguishers are required for cooking hazards with cooking appliances using cooking oil. Other hazards are required to have extinguishers matching the hazards, selected and installed in accordance with NFPA 10. (ROP 96-61)

Notification of AHJ When a System is Impaired (where required) (NEW)

- Text was added to 11.1.6.1 to mandate that the AHJ be notified where required. (ROP 96-62)

Solid Fuel Used For Flavoring (NEW)

- Requirements were added to 12.1.2 and 14.3.4 to allow solid fuel used for flavoring. (ROC 96-28 and ROC 96-34)

Wall Mounted Fan Sketch (NEW)

- A new sketch showing a wall mounted fan was added as Figure A.4.2(f) (ROP 96-75)

Duct Cleaning Frequency Text (Deleted)

- In A.11.6.2, the time reference was deleted as there is no such frequency for cleaning. Only a measurement of deposition is used to establish a trigger for cleaning. (ROP96-76)

References for Cooking Appliance Standards (NEW)

- New annex material was added as A.12.1.1 that provides useful information on the various cooking appliance standards. (ROP 96-78)

Duct Cleaning Personnel, Equipment and Recommendations (NEW)

- New advisory material was added for cleaning personnel including a list of recommended personal protective equipment. (ROC 96-35)

End of Editorial Comments

THIS PAGE HAS BEEN INTENTIONALLY LEFT BLANK

Chapter Three – Appliances

Cooking with different types of appliances; a griddle on the left and a solid fuel charbroiler on the right.

Appliances

Energy and Controls

In this chapter we review the energy sources, appliances, and the grease residues that are created from commercial cooking.

Just a few decades ago our grandparents, and even some of our parents, were restricted to using a couple of heating methods for cooking food. Today technological advances, along with imported cooking styles and ethnic diversity, have created an assortment of appliances and cooking methods.

Many of these new cooking trends in food preparation have increased the risk of fire in exhaust systems. There are a number of appliances that by virtue of their heating technique or mechanical operation may cause an instant and uncontrollable flash of flame that could touch off an exhaust system fire; particularly broilers and deep fat fryers.

Appliance Codes

NFPA 96 provides a number of standards that promote fire safety by proper placement of appliances in relation to the hood and/or grease removal devices (filters).

General NFPA 96 requirements from Sections 11 and 12 relating to appliances:[1]

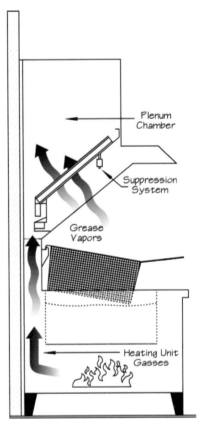

Flue gas exhaust bypass

- All equipment must be maintained in accordance with the requirements and standards during all periods of its operation.

- The distance between filters (grease removal devices) and the cooking surface shall be as great as possible but <u>not</u> less than 457.2 mm (18 in.) and 1.22 m (4 ft) for solid fuel appliances.

- Appliances without exposed flame and where flue gases exhaust (chimneys) bypass filters, the minimum vertical distance can be reduced to 152.4 mm (6 in.).

- Some listed appliances may be exempt from these distance requirements

- Filters must be in place and the exhaust fan operating whenever cooking equipment is turned on

- Appliances must be provided with means to ensure that they are returned to their proper location (under the fire extinguisher) after maintenance or cleaning (See Footnote)[2]

Appliances shall be approved based on one of the following criteria:

- Listed by a testing laboratory

- Test data acceptable to the authority having jurisdiction

- Instructions for manually operating the fire-extinguishing system shall be posted conspicuously in the kitchen and shall be reviewed with employees by the management

- Appliances shall not be operated while its fire-extinguishing system or exhaust system is nonoperational or otherwise impaired

---

[1] See NFPA 96, Sections 4.1, 6.2, 11.1 and 12.

[2] 11.1.6 Cooking equipment shall not be operated while its fire-extinguishing system or exhaust system is nonoperational or impaired.

11.1.6.1 Where the fire-extinguishing system or exhaust system is nonoperational or impaired, the systems shall be tagged noncompliant, and the owners or the owner's representative shall be notified in writing of the impairment.

- Appliances requiring protection shall not be moved, modified, or rearranged without prior reevaluation of the fire-extinguishing system by the system installer or servicing agent, unless otherwise allowed by the design of the fire-extinguishing system

- The fire-extinguishing system shall not require reevaluation where the cooking appliances are moved to perform maintenance and cleaning provided the appliances are returned to approved design location prior to cooking operations, and any disconnected fire-extinguishing system nozzles attached to the appliances are reconnected in accordance with the manufacturer's listed design manual

Appliance Docking

NFPA 96 12.1.2.3.1 An approved method shall be provided that will ensure that the appliance is returned to an approved design location.

There are several means of retaining appliances. However, the vast majority of applaince are not safely retained. This requirement assists in keeping the appliances under the range of the fire suppression heat detectors and nozzles.

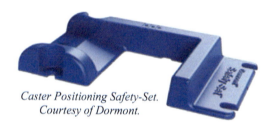

*Caster Positioning Safety-Set.
Courtesy of Dormont.*

An approved method must be provided that ensures the appliance is returned to an designated location

Cooking Energy Sources

The three primary sources of cooking energy are:

- **Gas** (natural gas or propane)

- **Electric** (assorted heating coils and elements)

- **Solid** (wood, charcoal, mesquite, pitch, etc.)

A typical gas cooking application

A typical electric cooking application

Hardwood used in solid fuel cooking

Gas

The fuel gases most commonly encountered in commercial kitchen fires are natural gas and commercial propane.

Natural Gas: Natural gas is a naturally occurring largely hydrocarbon gas product, often in association with crude petroleum. It accumulates in underground pockets and is recovered by drilling wells. There are no standards that specify its composition; natural gas is mostly methane, with lesser amounts of nitrogen, ethane, propane, and other traces. Natural gas is lighter than air. Its density is 0.59 to 0.719. Its ignition temperature is 482°C to 632°C (900°F to 1170°F).

Commercial Propane: Also known as liquefied petroleum (LP) gas, propane is derived from the refining of petroleum. Propane gas is heavier than air, with a vapor density of 1.5. Its ignition temperature is similar to natural gas, 493°C to 604°C (920°F to 1120°F).

Natural Gas Systems: One difference between natural gas systems and propane systems is that natural gas is piped directly to the consumer's building, whereas propane is typically stored in tanks on site. The major difference between the two gases is their energy content. A cubic foot of natural gas will produce about 1000 Btus, whereas a cubic foot of LP gas will produce 2500 Btus.

Natural gas and propane burn at temperatures in excess of 1871°C (3400°F). Auto ignition temperatures of lard or vegetable cooking oils are in the order of 273 to 420°C (523 to 788°F), so the boiling and splattering of oils onto live flames can result in instant ignition.

The installation and maintenance of fuel gas systems is covered in *NFPA 54, National Fuel Gas Code.*

Gas Temperature Controls

Appliance temperature controls may be fixed or interactive. An example of a fixed control is the burner control knob on range tops. Interactive controls generally consist of a reactive device, which undergoes some change in response to heat. This change then causes a switch to open or close. Examples of interactive controls are solenoids, relays and thermocouples such as those found in deep fryers.

The appliance must be listed or acceptable to the AHJ. They must also be installed in accordance with their listing. Appliances under the control of a thermostat are generally required to incorporate a backup thermostat in case the main thermostat fails.[3]

Certain safety devices are required on all gas appliances. Because of the danger of gas escaping unignited from a burner, gas appliances generally incorporate a pilot verification system. This system does not release gas to the main burner until the presence of an ignition source, or pilot is verified. This is generally accomplished with a thermocouple. A thermocouple is a device consisting of two different metal alloys that generate an electrical current when heated. (They convert heat energy to electrical energy). This electrical energy is used to power an electromagnet, which holds open a spring-loaded valve. When the pilot is not ignited, the electromagnet can no longer hold the valve open and the gas is stopped.

Electric Systems

Requirements for the design and installation of electrical appliances are found in NFPA 70, National Electrical Code, and in various Underwriters Laboratories standards.

Over time, wiring can become frayed and extremely brittle. Most electric appliances have thermostatic controls that can malfunction.

One way to keep your emergency lighting from getting greasy

---

[3] See NFPA 96, Chapter 12.

Solid Fuels

Solid fuel is defined as any solid, organic, consumable fuel such as briquettes, mesquite, hardwood, or charcoal. The most popular forms of solid fuel are briquettes or lump charcoal.

Solid fuel is unique because ash and unburned particles of wood/charcoal accumulate in the exhaust system at a prodigious rate. The ash readily mixes with the grease buildup to create large volumes of combustible residues. Buildup from solid fuel cooking can create a serious fire hazard in as little as a week.

This buildup quickly reduces the extraction efficiency of filters and increases static pressure.

Solid fuel cooking has the additional disadvantage of not having an automatic fuel shut off.

Natural lump charcoal comes in the irregular shapes of natural wood

Example of factory made briquettes

Natural Wood (not charcoal)

There are a number of regionally different solid fuels used for cooking and smoking food. In the Pacific Northwest, alder wood and bark are used to barbeque fish. In the South, pine resin is used for potatoes. Various specialty woods (hickory, oak, pecan, mesquite and others) are also used.

Requirements for Solid Fuel Cooking Operations

Although solid fuel cooking represents less than 1% of all cooking, because of the high volumes of ash and soot that will mix with the grease residues, NFPA 96, *Chapter 14 Solid Fuel Cooking Operations* was created. It requires that where solid fuel smoke and effluent escape the appliance, an exhaust system is to be provided.

Placing wood near gas burners is becoming a growing practice. This will create creosote and ash much like any solid fuel charbroiler.

Venting Application

Venting requirements of solid fuel cooking operations shall be in accordance with NFPA 96, Section 14.1:

- When a solid fuel cooking appliance is located in a space with other vented equipment, all vented equipment must have an exhaust system interlocked with a makeup air system

- When a solid fuel cooking appliance allows effluent to escape from its opening, the opening must be covered by a hood and exhaust system

- All solid fuel appliances need spark arresters to minimize the amount of sparks and embers in the ducts

- When a solid fuel appliance is not located under a hood (such as wood-burning pizza ovens), a spark arrester must be present to minimize the sparks and embers entering the chimneys and flues

Smoke flavoring is considered the same as being solid fuel. It should be treated the same way for fire protection because of the buildup of ash and creosote.

> *New 2011 NFPA 96, 14.3.4: Cooking processes, including but not limited to those that use any solid fuel for cooking enhancement or smoke flavoring, shall comply with 14.3.3. and 14.8.*

> *14.7.6 Fire-extinguishing equipment shall be rated and designed to extinguish solid fuel cooking fires.*

> *14.7.8* All solid fuel appliances (whether under a hood or not) with fire boxes of 0.14 m³ (5 ft³) volume or less shall have at least a listed 2-A rated water spray fire extinguisher or a 6 L (1.6 gal) wet chemical fire extinguisher listed for Class K fires in accordance with NFPA 10 with a maximum travel distance of 6 m (20 feet) to the appliance.*

For further details see Solid Fuel -- Key Changes to 2011 NFPA 96 in Chapter 2, Codes.

Location of Solid Fuel Appliances

Location of appliances shall be in accordance with NFPA 96, Section 14.2:

- All appliances must be located with respect to building construction and other construction so there is easy access to all appliances

- If solid fuel cooking appliances are listed for installation in confined spaces, it must be installed in accordance with the manufacturer's instructions[4]

- Solid fuel appliances cannot be installed in any location where gasoline or other flammable vapors are present

Hoods

Hoods shall be sized and located in a manner capable of capturing and containing all of the effluent discharging from the appliances. See NFPA 96, Section 14.3 for further details:

- The hood and exhaust serving solid fuel appliances shall comply with the requirements of NFPA 96, Chapters 5 through 10

- All solid fuel cooking equipment that has a hood and duct system must be separate from other exhaust systems

- Cooking equipment not requiring automatic fire-extinguishing equipment (microwave, steamers, and other non-grease producing appliances) can be installed under a hood with solid fuel cooking equipment as long as it is served by a duct system separate from the other exhaust systems

Exhaust for Solid Fuel Cooking

- Where solid fuel appliances require a natural draft, the vent shall comply with NFPA 96, Section 14.4

- A listed or approved grease duct system shall be provided for a solid fuel cooking exhaust system that is four stories in height or greater[5]

- Solid fuel exhaust systems cannot have wall terminations

Wood fired pizza oven. Generally these are cleaned as "wood chimneys."

---

[4] See NFPA 96, Section 14.2.3.

[5] See the Factory-Built Grease Ducts Section in Chapter 6, Ducts and Fans.

Grease Removal Devices

- Filters are required to be constructed of steel or stainless steel. Aluminum filters are not allowed.

- In solid fuel cooking, if sparks and embers are generated, spark arrester devices must be used prior to the grease removal device to minimize entrance into the hood and duct system

- Filters shall be a minimum of 1.2 m (4 ft) above the appliance cooking surface

Air Movement

- A makeup air system must be provided at all times during cooking operations to ensure a positive supply of replacement air

- Solid fuel cooking operations with makeup air systems must be interlocked with the exhaust air system and powered if necessary, to prevent negative pressure while the solid fuel appliance is in operation[6]

Fire-Extinguishing Equipment

Fire-extinguishing equipment for solid fuel cooking shall be installed and maintained in accordance with NFPA 96, Section 14.7:

- Solid fuel cooking appliances that produce grease-laden vapors, as well as grease removal devices, hoods and ducts must be protected by fire-extinguishing equipment

- Where acceptable to the AHJ solid fuel cooking appliances constructed of solid masonry, reinforced portland, or refractory cement concrete do not require fixed pipe automatic fire-extinguishing equipment

- Listed fire-extinguishing equipment for solid fuel burning cooking appliances, shall comply with NFPA 96, Chapter 10 and shall be comprised of water-based agents

- Fire-extinguishing equipment must be rated and designed to extinguish solid fuel cooking fires in the entire hazard area and prevent reignition of the fuel in accordance with the manufacturers' recommendations

Inspection, Cleaning, and Maintenance for Solid Fuel Cooking

Solid fuel cooking appliances must be inspected, cleaned and maintained in accordance with NFPA 96, Chapter 11:

- The combustion chamber (flue or chimney) needs to be cleaned and inspected weekly for residues, corrosion and physical damage

- Any deterioration or defect that might weaken the chamber must be immediately repaired

Two ducts serving solid fuel cooking. Courtesy of Bryan Exhaust Service.

---

[6] See NFPA 96, Section 14.6.3.

Fuel Storage, Handling, and Ash Removal for Solid Fuel Cooking

Fuel Storage, Handling, and Ash Removal requirements must be in accordance with NFPA 96, Section 14.9:

- Solid fuel appliances are to be installed on noncombustible materials that extend 91.4 cm (3 ft) around the appliance

- Combustible and limited combustible surfaces within 91.4 cm (3 ft) of the sides or 1.83 m (6 ft) above solid fuel cooking appliance must be protected in a manner acceptable to the AHJ

- Solid fuel cooking appliances that are specifically listed for less clearance to combustibles shall be permitted to be installed in accordance with the requirements of the listing and the manufacturers' instructions

A pile of solid fuel outside a restaurant kitchen

Solid Fuel Storage

- No more than a 1-day supply of fuel should be stored in the same room as the appliance

- Fuel is not to be stored above any appliance or closer than 91.4 cm (3 ft) to any portion of an appliance constructed of metal or any other appliance that could ignite the fuel, unless in a listed or approved device

- Fuel storage areas must have a sprinkler system meeting the requirements of NFPA 13 and acceptable to the AHJ

Solid Fuel Handling and Ash Removal

- Solid fuel must be ignited with a match or an approved built in gas flame or other approved ignition source

- Ash, cinders, and other fire debris must be removed from the firebox on regular intervals to prevent interference with the draft and minimize the length of time the access door is open

- Ash must be removed from the chamber at least once a day

- All ash must be watered down before removal in order to extinguish hot ash or cinders when the ash is moved

- A water supply with a flexible hose must be provided at the solid fuel appliance to cool a fire that has become too hot or to cool hot embers before leaving the premises

- For appliances with fireboxes no bigger then 1.5 m^2 (5 ft^3) the water source is permitted to be a 37.9 L (10 gal) container with a hand pump

- The nozzle must be fitted with a manual shutoff device and must provide a fine to medium spray that can reach all areas of the combustion chamber and cooking chamber

- A minimum of 16 gauge steel container or cart with a lid must be used to remove the ash

- The ash removal container must not exceed a 75.7 L (20 gal) capacity and must only be used for that purpose. It shall be constructed in such a way as to be easy to use by any employee and must be able to pass through any passageway.

- The ash shall be carried to a separate heavy metal container (or dumpster) used exclusively for the purpose

Mesquite being heated over a gas range burner

Other Safety Requirements

- All solid fuel cooking appliances that are site-built must be submitted for approval by the AHJ before they are installed

- All units submitted to the AHJ must be installed, operated and maintained in accordance with the terms of the manufacturers' instructions and any requirements of the AHJ

- Other than the spark arrester required, there must not be any additional devices of any type in any portion of the appliance or its exhaust system

- Solid fuel exhaust systems shall be separate from all other exhaust systems. Where there is a solid fuel appliance, it must be served by exhaust systems with an interlock with the makeup air system. The purpose of the interlock is to prevent the space from attaining a negative pressure while the solid fuel appliance is in operation.

- Hoods must be capable of capturing all smoke and grease vapor from the solid fuel appliance. These are usually canopy hoods as the filters are required to be 121.9 cm (48 in.) away from the appliance. Solid fuel appliances must have approved fire-extinguishing systems over both the appliance and in the hood and duct system.

- Listed steel spark arrest filters are required to minimize sparks and embers from entering the hood. Filters shall be a minimum of 1.2 m (4 ft) above the appliance cooking surface.

Appliances Types

Below is a list of common heat-producing appliances encountered in commercial kitchens:

- Solid Fuel Charbroilers
- Gas Fueled Charbroilers
- Gas Chain Broilers
- Electric Fueled Charbroilers
- Salamanders and Upright Broilers
- Griddles

- Conveyor Ovens
- Deep Fat Fryers
- Oriental Woks
- Stove Tops (Open burners)
- Ovens

Charbroilers

Gas burners heat ceramic or volcanic briquettes that radiate heat upward to stationary grids that hold product. Metal (cast) or stainless steel radiants are also used. The grid produces cosmetic markings on the food. Melting fat drips on the briquettes and burns, creating very high accumulations of both grease and ash. Although the volume of grease and ash buildup is not as large as solid fuel these combustibles still clog filters, coat hoods and ducts, and can create a carbon buildup on and around the appliances.

Gas Chain Broilers

These units are popular for broiling hamburgers in fast food restaurants.

Most broilers are divided into two sections. Food moves by conveyor chain through a cooking chamber where infrared, convection and conduction heat may be used. The oven utilizes a high-speed fan to distribute heat through air distribution plates. Due to the high fat content (up to 30%) intense broiling of hamburgers creates large amounts of grease runoff.

The broiler area must be kept free of combustible materials and the flow of combustion and ventilation air must not be obstructed.

Chain broilers come in a number of makes and models. Obtain a copy of the Owner's Manual for specific details.

An example of solid fuel charbroiler

Examples of chain broilers used to cook hamburgers

Catalytic Converter

Often this type of broiler will employ a catalytic converter to reduce smoke and grease output. The drawback is catalytic converters can increase exhaust duct temperatures by up to 93°C (200°F). If the exhaust system isn't being cleaned often enough, liquefied grease can drain down the duct and cause an immediate fire hazard.

Electric Charbroilers

An electric charbroiler, while not a great producer of ash and embers, will create a large amount of grease runoff depending on the type, quality, and quantity of meats cooked. These oils will condense and buildup under and around the appliance and on overhead surfaces.

Salamander and Upright Broiler

Radiant heat is generated by gas fired ceramic or infrared burners at approximately 871°C (1600°F). The heat is radiated downward onto a grid where the food product rests. The grid may be raised or lowered and rolled in or out.

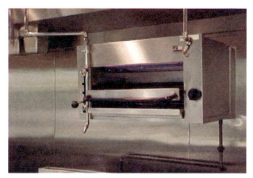

A salamander broiler

An upright broiler

In many cases, these broilers are located too close to the filters or the trough of the hood where grease will accumulate. If there is a fire in the salamander flames can quickly escape out the gas flue chimney and ignite grease on the filters or the lower section of the hood.

Additionally, heat from the gas flue chimneys will bake grease onto the hood and filters. In some kitchens the placement of the salamander makes it very difficult to remove filters, thereby reducing the frequency of cleanings.

NFPA 96, Section 6.2.2 addresses separation distances between salamanders and grease removal devices (filters).

Filters need to be 457mm (18 in) away from the flue gas outlet or direct flames

A stainless steel baffle placed <u>at least</u> 152.4 mm (6 in) from the filters can be used.

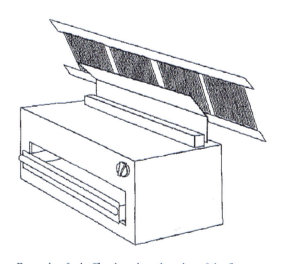

Example of a baffle placed on the edge of the flue gas exhaust that will deflect heat and flames from the filters. NFPA 96 2011 Fig. A.6.2.2.2

Demonstating how the shelf slides in and out of a Salamander (as opposed to a fixed shelf "Cheese Melter")

Looking up into the upper broiler heat element. These elements will plug due to the spitting of meats and other products being cooked, resulting in reduced efficiency and combustible buildup.

View of top of a typical salamander. Flue gas exhaust at back

Cheese Melter

A cheese melter is a downsized version of a salamander but for low volume applications, however, it can be just as dangerous. The most common difference between a salamander and a cheese melter is the salamander has a "rollout" (or slide out) rack and the cheese melter has a stationary rack.

Griddle Top Cooking

The popularity of flat griddle cooking in North American culture creates very high volumes of grease, particularly in major fast food chains.

A griddle is a flat 19 mm to 25.4 mm (3/4 in. to 1 in.) thick steel plate that is under-fired by rows of thermostatically controlled gas burners. Griddles operate at lower temperatures than charbroilers, normally between 149° and 177°C (300° and 351°F). When hamburgers, sausages, or steaks are regularly cooked on this appliance large amounts of grease vapors are produced.

A grooved griddle is a slightly sloping plate of solid steel with raised ridges. The ridges are designed to give steaks and fish the cosmetic markings of a charbroiler without the smoke or ash.

Grooved griddles are heated by electric or gas burners. The grease created is similar to a flat surface griddle.

Conveyor Ovens

Some conveyor ovens are designed to cook pizzas but will also cook a number of other foods, such as chicken wings, which produce grease. Most authorities agree that these units must be under proper Type I systems with fire-extinguishing systems.

An electric motor drives a chain conveyor similar to a chain broiler. Food passes heat (usually gas) elements.

 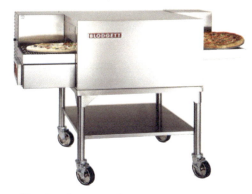

Types of conveyor ovens. These units are capable of cooking more than just pizzas.

Oriental Woks

In the hands of an experienced chef a wok is a very versatile appliance. It can be used to deep fry, boil water, skillet fry, stir-fry, or stew.

Because woks burn so hot they quickly vaporize the oils in the foods cooked (mostly vegetables). These vaporized oils tend to rapidly recondense in the hood and surrounding areas.

Woks have a gas flue chimney similar to all gas appliances, therefore posing the same ignition risk.

Most woks have no thermostat to control temperature. The cook controls the heat. If left unattended with oil in the wok, ignition can take place.

Cooking with a wok

Looking at the burner beneath the wok

Gas flue chimney

Oriental cooking grease accumulation

Open Burner Ranges and Ovens

An open burner range is a standard appliance in almost all kitchens and is a versatile and adaptable piece of equipment. Hot top and closed (flat) top ranges burn hotter and allow for multiple pots and pans to be placed on top. The fuel flow rate and heat intensity is usually controlled with the burner fuel supply valve. Open burners have 20,000 BTU's of instant input per burner. Flare-ups are very common on these units.

Ignition of the fuel in a gas range or oven can result from a standing pilot flame or electrical device that produces an arc or glow for ignition.

In the oven, a thermostat and a valve on the fuel or switch power supply controls the interior temperature.

Fires can take place when combustible products spill over and run down into the combustion chamber or if there is a malfunction in the thermostat, valve, or piping.

Example of open burner range tops

Example of open burner range tops

Deep Fat Fryers

There are two primary types of commercial deep fat fryers: pressure and open.

Both types of fryers will produce large amounts of soft grease buildup in the exhaust system when used to cook freshly breaded (floured) products (such as fresh fish and chicken). When used to cook frozen products particularly those containing sugar (such as pies, fries and meats) a thin but very hard layer of "shellac-like" grease will build up on the hood and duct.

Deep fryers require a separate high limit control in addition to the adjustable operating control (thermostat) to shut off fuel when the oil temperature reaches 246°C (475°F).[7]

---

[7] See NFPA 96, Section 12.2.

Pressure Fryers

A pressure fryer is an airtight kettle that traps vapors from the cooking oil and increases the pressure inside the kettle. In an open fryer, because of its high water content, food never heats higher than 100°C (212°F) internally, regardless of cooking oil temperature. In a pressure fryer, the temperature increases 3°F for each pound of pressure.

Oil pressure cooker

Open Fryers

An open fryer is a vat or multiple vats heated by burners running through tubes underneath the vat. The tubes may serve as a heat exchanger for a gas burner, or may contain electric coils. Baskets of food are submerged in cooking oil heated from 163°C to 191°C (325°F to 375°F).

Normal cooking temperature for deep fryer vegetable oil is about 191°C (375°F). At 218°C (424°F) oil starts to smoke. Smoke production will increase as the temperature rises. Auto ignition takes place at approximately 273° to 420°C (523° to 788°F). This auto ignition temperature will vary primarily because of the type and amount of impurities in the oil.

The two primary fire threats from deep fryers are thermostat malfunction and grease residues building up in the gas flue chimney.

NFPA 96 requires a clearance of at least 406 mm (16 in.) between fryers and any open flame burners. A 203 mm (8 in.) metal or tempered glass panel can be used to achieve this clearance.

New "high-temperature" fryers are designed to maintain the heat of the oil longer and cook at higher temperatures (much closer to autoignition), making these units a more significant fire risk. Appliance manufacturers should be involved in notifying end-users that new 'high-temp' fryers require upgraded fire-extinguishing systems.

Note: Some of these fire safety concerns were the primary reasons behind the need for the new UL 300 (ULC 1254.6) *Standard for Fire Testing of Fire Extinguishing Systems for Protection of Restaurant Cooking Areas (1996).*[8]

A row of deep fat fryers

---

[8] See Chapter 5, Fire-Extinguishing Systems.

Fryer Operation

Open fryers are particularly susceptible to poor mechanical maintenance. Thermostats and shut-off relays that are not properly maintained can fail, resulting in the burners continuing to heat the oil to autoignition temperatures.

Most fryers operate with two capillary type thermostats. These consist of a sealed reservoir of fluid (usually xylene) connected to a diaphragm and switch by a narrow copper tube. As the temperature increases, the liquid expands, causing movement of the diaphragm, which, in turn, pushes on a small switch and opens a set of contacts and shuts down the burners.

In gas units, these contacts are in series with the pilot verification thermocouple. Opening the contacts de-energizes the electromagnet and a spring closes the main gas valve.

The capillary tubes are subject to breaking when the fryer is cleaned. When that happens, the fluid leaks out, and the thermostat no longer responds to heat. The fryer will keep working, because the contacts will stay closed. The temperature is then under the control of the high limit thermostat. The oil may smoke, but many restaurant operators will keep on cooking. If the high limit switch were to fail, there will be a fire.

In some fryers, the high limit thermostat will include a "negative biased" reservoir that is slightly below atmospheric pressure, so that if the capillary tube breaks, the loss of negative pressure will open the circuit. The fryer cannot operate in this condition; however, it takes only a minute to bypass the safety by moving the wire from the terminal at one side of the microswitch to the other side. If it is the high limit capillary that breaks first, and it is tampered with, the operating thermostat will control the oil temperature until the second capillary breaks. Then there is no control to stop the burners from continuing to operate. This will result in autoignition of the cooking oil.

There must be a 16" gap between the fryer and any open flame. This can be achieved with a spacer (8" and 8").

Fryer Chimney Grease Buildup

In nearly all fryer designs, the flue gas exhaust vent for the heat from the burner elements (whether gas or electric) goes up the back of the unit behind the vat. With repeated splashing a substantial coating of grease can build up and harden on top of and around this exhaust stack (like creosote in a wood burning chimney). This residue provides an excellent fuel source especially if some of the buildup falls close to the burner elements below. Most new fryers are constructed with the chimney open at the bottom, so any debris that falls down the gas flue chimney should fall straight to the floor.

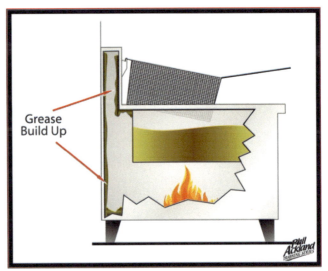

Grease Build Up

Illustration of how grease can accumulate in the flue gas exhaust of a typical deep fryer.

Non-Compliant Appliances

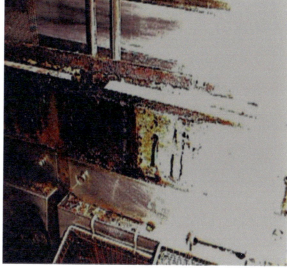

Counter-clockwise from top right:

A fire in the chimney of a deep fryer because of grease accumulation

A leaking valve created a fire hazard

A deep fryer right next to open flame

The deep fryers are outside of the hood and fire suppression coverage

The rock is holding the gas valve open, but the greasy rag (wick) keeps the rock from scratching the fryer

A missing grease cup just above the deep fryers flue gas exhaust. This will lead to grease from the hood trough dripping down the flue gas exhaust vent to the live flame of the burners.

A charbroiler under a galley hood. There must be 48 inches between the highest point of the charbroiler and the closest point of the filter.

The top of a salamander that is too close to the filters. If there is a flare up in the salamander the flames will be drawn right into the hood and a fire will not be easily seen for quick action.

More than 15 gallons of cooking oil stored on an operating salamander! Enough said.

Cooking By-Products

During cooking, oils and fats change from a solid or semi-solid state into a liquid form. They then atomize and form grease-laden vapors, or drain off in the form of altered oils. These grease vapors contain water molecules in the form of steam, mixed with evaporated fats and oils. Particles of this mixture are called aerosols. These aerosols are carried from the cooking surface into the hood by the negative pressure created by the ventilation system and thermal currents created by cooking appliances. This generates a plume or rising cloud of grease and smoke.

The higher the cooking surface temperature becomes, the more grease is transformed into a vapor state. As this vapor cools, it condenses or returns to a solid state (although chemically altered). This grease residue (altered oils) is combustible. Its ignition temperatures are slightly below the average ignition temperature of the original cooking oil. So, instead of exhausting the grease hazard, the exhaust system actually becomes a fire hazard.

The combination of various appliances, different food products and the ways in which they are cooked will produce an array of grease residues.[9]

---

[9] For information on cleaning exhaust systems, see the Kitchen Exhaust System Cleaners Section in Chapter 7, Service Providers.

An Inspector needs to encourage restaurants to stay on a regular cleaning schedule, so that the buildup does not become too great.

From a practical perspective, grease generation falls into two essential categories: stir-fry/deep-fry versus element cooked (i.e. broilers, grills, stovetops, etc.). The following is a generally accepted chart that ranks cooking styles and grease accumulation, in order of volume. Average surface temperatures of these appliances are also listed.

Plenum area of a hood. The fire-extinguishing system link and nozzle are covered with grease.

Dirty and leaking sections of ducts

Grease Accumulation Severity

Element Cooking:

Severity	Product	Fuel	Approximate Appliance Temperature
1	Fish - especially salmon and halibut	Mesquite charbroilers	816 - 1093°C (1500 - 2000°F)
2	Steaks - beef, pork, lamb	Mesquite charbroilers	816 - 1093°C (1500 - 2000°F)
3	Hamburgers	Mesquite charbroilers	816 - 1093°C (1500 - 2000°F)
4	Steaks - beef, pork, lamb	Charbroiler	816°C (1500°F)
5	Hamburgers	Charbroiler	816°C (1500°F)
6	Hamburgers	On a grooved grill	260° - 316°C (500 - 600°F)
7	Bacon / sausage	On a flat grill	191°C (375°F)
8	Other cooking	Elec./gas ovens and steamers	99°C (210°F)

Stir/Deep-Fried:

Severity	Product	Fuel	Approximate Appliance Temperature
1	High tech fat fryers	Gas	316°C (600°F)
2	Breaded - chicken or fish	Gas	191°C (375°F)
3	Oriental wok	Gas	260°C (500°F)
4	Frozen - French fries or pies	Gas	191°C (375°F)

Charts courtesy of R.J.Reynolds Inc.

Also see NFPA 96, Table 11.4 Schedule of Inspection for Grease Buildup.

Solid Fuel Cooked/Charbroiler Grease

Solid fuel poses the additional problem of ash that mixes with the grease to create unusually large volumes of buildup. Solid fuel cooking/charbroiling meats normally cooked are: beef steaks, burgers and fish.

Charbroiling meats creates high volumes of grease. Initially, a dry but adhesive stain (like a nicotine stain) forms directly against the metal surface. On top of this staining, layers of thick, heavy, black carbon will build up. It is not unusual to encounter accumulations of grease 19 mm to 25.4 mm thick (3/4 in. to 1 in.) on vertical surfaces and along the inside top of horizontal ducting. Where systems are not regularly cleaned, as much as 7.5 cm (3 in.) of grease can accumulate on the bottom of horizontal duct sections.[10]

Examples of grease created by solid fuel cooking

Deep Fryer Grease

Deep frying creates grease that is very much like translucent creosote. When there is a large amount of water in the foods cooked, as in the case of frozen food, the buildup can have an almost shiny appearance. It is as hard as multiple layers of shellac.

High volume grease producing foods include: potatoes (starch), sugar based foods (i.e. pies and turnovers, sugar = carbon) and frozen products (ice = moisture). Fresh breaded foods such as battered chicken or fish can create large volumes of rather soft (flour filled) grease.

Examples of grease created by a donut maker

  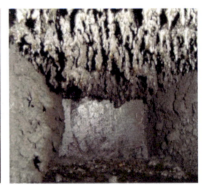

Examples of grease created by deep fryer cooking

---

[10] For more details, see the Solid Fuel Section in this Chapter.

Wok Grease

The nature of wok cooking creates grease that is a very sticky, syrup-like liquid, having a consistency between honey and molasses. Once this grease residue has set on a metal surface for some time and has been exposed to temperature changes, it becomes extremely adhesive, with a flexible caramel-like consistency. The surface tension cannot be broken by normal scraping or with general purpose cleaning chemicals. After a further length of time it becomes dry and hard, similar to tar. This type of grease can readily plug up the pull cable of the fire-extinguishing system.

Examples of grease created by wok style cooking

Gourmet charbroiler hamburger cooking

Oriental cooking with water wash hoods

Open access door of solid fuel (steak)

Deep fried breaded seafood

THIS PAGE HAS BEEN INTENTIONALLY LEFT BLANK

Chapter Four – Hoods

Hoods

Hoods, the most visible component of a commercial kitchen ventilation system, capture heat and effluents in the thermal plume rising off the top of cooking equipment. The hood is the primary filtration system, the size and make depending on the number and type of cooking appliances used. All Type I hoods contain baffle filters, modular extractors, filtration or cyclic water wash systems.

In theory, the closer the hood is to the cooking surfaces the more efficiently it will draw. However, this efficiency is very dependant on the draw of the fan.

A Fire Inspector checking behind the filters for grease buildup

A typical hood in a Burger King restaurant

Steam and smoke being captured by the hood

Type I Hood

Type I Hoods

Hoods may or may not be listed. However, unlisted hoods must meet the criteria of applicable national and local codes. Air requirements are based on the square footage of the hood capture area. These air requirements are generally higher than for listed hoods.[1] Fire actuated dampers are not permitted in unlisted hoods. Unlisted hoods are usually built locally by HVAC shops and need careful inspection when installed.[2] Listed hoods are generally classified as hoods with or without dampers.

---

[1] See ASHRAE STANDARD 154.

[2] For more information on hood and duct construction, see SMACNA *Installation of Commercial Kitchen Exhaust and Makeup Air Systems* Manual.

All Type I hoods must have the following features:

- Continuously welded, liquid tight seams
- Acceptable clearances from combustibles
- Ability to capture all grease vapors
- Suspension by noncombustible hangers
- Supports strong enough to handle load bearing items such as grease buildup and personnel working on the system
- Accessibility for cleaning and inspection
- Penetrations in hoods must be sealed in an approved manner, particularly piping for the fire-extinguishing system
- Painted hoods are allowed

Type I Listed Hoods

Listed hoods are constructed and installed in accordance with the manufacturers' listing.

- Listed hoods must meet UL Standard 710 or equivalent[3]
- They may contain dampers and automatic wash-down (water wash) systems
- They will contain a permanent tag that defines related performance criteria
- Listed hoods are generally more energy efficient. Air requirements are based on length. There is no consequence for a deeper (wider) hood that affords improved capture as the overhang increases.

According to IMC single island hoods must overhang the cooking equipment by a minimum of 15.2 cm (6 in.) on all four sides of the hood. However, it is recommended that the overhang be extended to 30.5 cm (12 in.). It is also recommended that there is a minimum overhang of 15.2 to 30.5 cm (6 to 12 in.) beyond the widest cooking appliance for the front.

Both IMC and ASHRAE state that greater overhangs (reaching 30.5 cm or 12 in.) will increase capture and containment.

Two examples of canopy hoods with baffle filters

---

[3] For recommended flow rates, ASHRAE STANDARD 154.

Components of the Exhaust Hood

Common components of the canopy exhaust hood design are:

- Trough
- Plenum chamber
- Inside of hood
- Fire-Extinguishing System
- Outside of hood

- Duct collar
- Grease drip pan
- Baffle Filter or Cartridge
- Dampers (only in listed hoods)

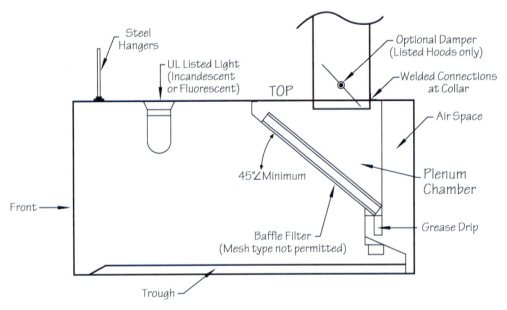

Graphic example of generic components of a canopy style hood. Not to scale.

Common Hood Designs

Canopy Hoods

The names hood, canopy or ventilator can be used to describe a canopy hood.

The three primary designs of canopy hoods are:

- Wall mounted (most familiar type against a wall)
- Single island (open on four sides with a single line of cooking equipment)
- Double island (open on four sides with cooking equipment back to back)

Note: The three examples listed above are considered "canopy" style hoods. The canopy name is often incorrectly associated with "proximity" (aka galley or backshelf) and "eyebrow" (oven) hoods.

Two examples of canopy style hoods

All canopy hoods must be mounted a minimum of 198 cm (6 ft. – 6 in.) above the finished floor as required by NFPA 96. They may be mounted higher for design considerations but generally require an increase in the amount of exhaust air to function properly.

Canopy hoods are sized in such a way that the perimeter of the hood ideally overlaps the area that the appliances occupy. This forms an envelope for grease-laden vapor to rise into and then be pulled out of the building by the exhaust fan.

Filtration in the hood is provided either singularly or in combination of filters, baffles or continuous water misting.

Single Island Hoods

A single island hood is used over one row of cooking equipment placed where no walls exist. These hoods are generally sized larger and use more airflow than a wall canopy hood with the same cooking battery.

Island hoods (both single and double island) are more susceptible to cross drafts, heat and air spillage because all four sides are exposed. Island hoods are dependent on the thermal updraft of appliance heat and the energy of the exhaust fan to remove contaminated air from the hood.

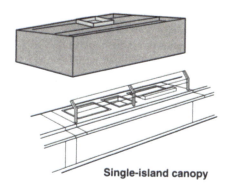

Single-island canopy

Double Island Hoods

A double island hood is used when two rows of cooking equipment, open on four sides, are placed back to back. A configuration of two wall canopy hoods placed back to back or a larger single island hood with a "V" pattern of filters can be used. The same overhang requirements apply as for other hoods.

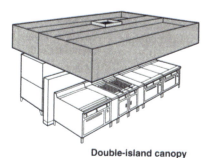

Double-island canopy

Wall Canopy Hoods

The wall canopy hood is used when the cooking equipment is placed against a wall. Hoods that are used against a wall have a tendency to capture and contain the effluent using less airflow than in an island type application. The wall will cause makeup air to enter at the front and sides of the hood, creating a front-to-rear airflow pattern. A primary issue with wall canopy hoods is the construction material of the wall.[4]

It is not recommended that a wall canopy hood be installed as a single island hood.

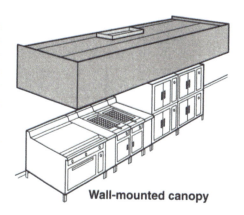

Wall-mounted canopy

Makeup Air Components of Canopy Hoods

Some canopy hoods, usually listed, will come with built in makeup air components. These are sometimes called Compensating Hoods. They are connected to the HVAC ducting to direct air into the kitchen in a prescribed manner according to the designer's specifications.

---

[4] See the Clearances to Combustibles Section in Chapter 6, Ducts and Fans.

Replacement air can be provided via four different internal methods through compensating hoods:

1. Air Curtain

2. Back Wall Discharge

3. Perimeter Discharge

4. Internal Discharge, AKA Short Circuit Hoods

Note: Short circuit hoods became popular some thirty years ago. The design was strongly marketed by manufacturers claiming energy savings. However, the design in recent years has been proven to be ineffective and energy wasting in spite of its claims. Some national chains are now retrofitting short circuit hoods and reporting significant energy savings. The retrofit is accomplished by eliminating the internal supply air connection making the hood an exhaust only to save fan energy and reduce maintenance. A test and balance must be included as part of this procedure.

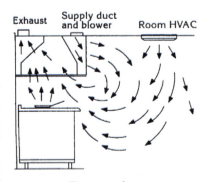

Front panel type

Drawings courtesy of Garland

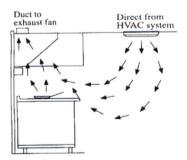

Makeup air supplied direct from HVAC system

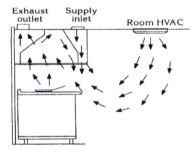

Integrated system, down discharge type

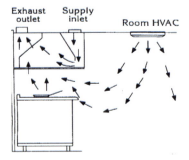

Short cycle type

Galley (Backshelf)

Also named "proximity" hoods, which refers to the close location of the hood with respect to the cooking equipment. These hoods are able to capture the contaminated air due to their close proximity. However, large surges of contaminated air can escape from the hood. This hood style is best suited for light and medium duty cooking applications such as griddles.

Actual distance from the cooking equipment varies between manufacturers depending on their UL listing. However proximity hoods are typically mounted at 25.4 to 91.4 cm (10 to 36 in.) above the appliance. Appliances usually extend past the face of the hood creating an underhang; therefore many types of appliance and cooking style are not suitable for proximity hoods.

Examples of galley style hoods over a cooking line of deep fat fryers

Flue Bypass Proximity Hoods

Because proximity hoods are mounted closer to the cooking equipment the grease filters are subject to abnormal heating loads from appliance flues. Additionally, gas-fired cooking equipment with flues will create heat from the flue that will radiate off the filters. To avoid these conditions flue bypass proximity hoods were developed. These hoods allow for the appliance flue gas outlets (chimneys) to be placed behind the filters. As heat buildup is reduced airflow requirements can be lowered.

Flue bypass is recommended for fryers and griddles.

Caution: The appliances must be correctly matched to the hood to ensure the placement of the flue outlet and proper capture of the cooking vapors.

Galley Hoods Over Charbroilers

Standard galley hoods cannot be used over charbroilers since they pose a serious fire hazard. Charbroilers require a 121.9 cm (48 in.) clearance between the cooking surface and the bottom edge of the filter. Specially designed listed galley hoods are occasionally allowed over charbroilers.

Non-Typical or Specialty Hood Designs

A third group exists that include:

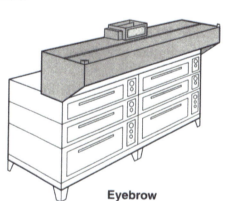

Eyebrow

- Eyebrow Hoods

- Pass-over Hoods

- Down Draft Appliance Systems

- Ventilated Ceiling Exhaust

- Recirculating Hoods or Ventless Systems

Eyebrow Hoods

Eyebrow hoods are designed to fit over the front of larger ovens and dishwashers. This hood is usually placed over appliances, which only produce heat and odor (non-grease producing). For complete capture and containment, overhang should be measured with the oven door open.

> *NFPA 96, Section 5.1.8.1: Eyebrow-type hoods over gas or electric ovens shall be permitted to have a duct constructed as required in Chapter 7 (of NFPA 96) from the oven flue(s) connected to the hood canopy upstream of the exhaust plenum as shown in Figure 5.1.8.1.*
>
> *5.1.8.2 The duct connecting the oven flue(s) to the hood canopy shall be connected with a continuous weld or have a duct-to-duct connection. [Figure 8.1.2.2(b) through Figure 8.1.2.2(d).]*

Pass-over Hoods

Found often in short order restaurants, pass-over hoods are built low to the cooking surface. The duct is normally out of view and runs down and then horizontally or may rise up at one end.

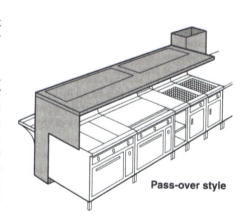

Pass-over style

As there is no ducting running vertically up from the hood, these hoods have the design benefit of not obstructing the view between the cooking operation and the waiters. Air is directed into the ducting at the back of the hood, the draw of the fan pulls it down the wall to either the basement area or to an underground shaft. From this point it runs to a junction where it then goes up, along a back wall, to the roof and fan. The distinct disadvantage of these systems is that they accumulate a much greater amount of grease because it collects easily in the lower areas.

The fire-extinguishing system must be installed in accordance with the manufacturer's listing.

Two examples of pass-over exhaust systems

Down Draft Appliance Systems

The designation "down draft" system has recently been given to tabletop cooking units. Traditionally these cooking units feature an integrated burner (gas or electric) built into the tabletop. Around the cooking unit is a space where the hot air and cooking vapors are pulled down into a duct filter arrangement and then directed out of the building.

These units may be installed in series; so multiple ducts could be connected to one larger duct. An inspector needs to confirm that proper access is supplied in the duct and at the fan. There may be a 'trapped area' at the bottom of the duct that contains a grease reservoir not exceeding 3.8 L (1 gal). (NFPA 96 7.1.4.2)

> *NFPA 96, Section 15.1* General Requirements. Down draft appliance ventilation systems containing or for use with appliances used in process producing smoke or grease-laden vapors shall be equipped with components complying with the following:*
>
> *(1) The clearance requirements of Section 4.2*
>
> *(2) The primary collection means designed for collecting cooking vapors and residues complying with the requirements of Chapter 5*
>
> *(3) Grease removal devices complying with Chapter 6*
>
> *(4) Special-purpose filters as listed in accordance with UL 1046*
>
> *(5) Exhaust ducts complying with Chapter 7*
>
> *(6) The air movement requirements of 8.2.1.2 and 8.2.2.3*
>
> *(7) Auxiliary equipment (such as particulate and odor removal devices) complying with Chapter 9*
>
> *(8) Fire-extinguishing equipment complying with the requirements of Chapter 10 and as specified in Section 15.2*
>
> *(9) The use and maintenance requirements of Chapter 11*
>
> *(10) The minimum safety requirements of Chapter 12*
>
> *15.2.1 A listed down draft appliance ventilation system employing an integral fire-extinguishing system including detection systems that has been evaluated for grease and smoke capture, fire-extinguishing and detection shall be considered as complying with Section 15.2.*

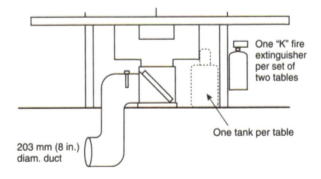

One "K" fire extinguisher per set of two tables

One tank per table

203 mm (8 in.) diam. duct

Ventilated Ceiling Exhaust

Ventilated ceiling exhaust systems were approved by ULC in 2004 and in 2005 by ETL. This type of exhaust system has been in use in Europe for many years. It is listed for light to medium duty only.

For further details see Key Changes in Chap 2 Codes.

Ultra Violet Light Technology

The latest technology in the hood filtration field is the use of ultra violet light. This process known as cold combustion breaks down organic compounds (grease vapors). The reaction converts the grease into carbon dioxide, water vapor and ozone. This process eliminates both grease and odor.

Ventilated Ceiling Exhaust

The principle behind these units is called Photolysis and Ozonolysis.

Photolysis: A chemical reaction produced by exposure to light or ultraviolet radiation.

Ozonolysis: A reaction that breaks down molecular structures.

Ultra violet light bulbs are placed within the plenum directly behind removable extractors. As grease laden air passes around the UV bulbs, usually arranged in a set of four or five, a chemical reaction takes place changing the grease to a fine white or gray powder. To oversimplify the process, the grease particles get "zapped."

This is a class of hoods that is gaining recognition for its ability to significantly reduce grease deposits within the duct and fan system.

These units come in canopy and galley hood design and some have water wash features.

Examples of a Ventmaster Ultraviolet Hood

Note: Behind the removable extractor there is an expanded metal screening device. This breaks down larger particles so they can be more easily dealt with by the UV light. These screens should not be confused with mesh filters (which are not allowed).

> *5.5.1 Duct systems connected to Ultraviolet Hoods shall comply with Chapter 7 (Ducts).*

There have been several installations where the ductwork has been light-weight steel instead of that called for by the NFPA 96 Standard. This is putting too much reliance on the ability of the UV and maintenance staff to keep the UV system running properly.

Examples of Ultraviolet tubes

Staff Maintenance

The kitchen staff should carry out maintenance of the cartridges and particle-separators during their routine cleaning program (put through the dishwasher or cleaned in the pot sink).

The UV lamps (cassettes) shall be cleaned on a quarterly basis by factory approved service technicians (depending on the type and volume of cooking).

Recirculating Hoods or Ventless Systems

Self-contained cooking equipment or kiosk ventilation systems, also called "recirculating hood systems" or "ventless fryers," require no ducting to the outside of the building. They are used in limited applications in light to medium duty cooking. They are tested to remove grease, smoke and odor from the plume and return the air to the same space or other areas within the building. These listed systems are specifically designed to work with a designated particular piece of equipment (usually a deep fryer).

The construction and internal filtration components of these systems allow them to be listed for use in a number of areas where the construction of fixed ventilation systems is either impossible or impractical, such as at temporary stadium or convention events.

The recirculating style hood includes the following:

- Grease removal devices such as a typical baffle filter
- A secondary HEPA filter or electrostatic precipitator
- Odor control device (generally charcoal)
- An exhaust fan

Giles Ventless Fryer
Courtesy of Giles Industries

When installed over approved cooking appliances, the components of a ventless hood system are designed to remove the grease vapors and objectionable odors created during cooking. The hood system performs this function through the use of a series of filters, maintained in a pressure-tight plenum chamber.

There are a number of safety interlocks, which sound alarms and shut down the cooking elements if any part of the filtration system is plugged or missing.

Type I Hoods - Construction Requirements

NFPA 96, Chapter 5.1 provides construction requirements for Type I hoods.

- The hood shall be constructed of and supported by steel not less than 1.09 mm (0.043 in.) (No. 18 MSG) in thickness, stainless steel not less than 0.94 mm (0.037 in.) (No. 20 MSG) in thickness, or other approved material of equivalent strength and fire and corrosion resistance
- All seams, joints, and penetrations shall have a liquidtight continuous external weld to the hood's lower outermost perimeter
- Seams, joints, and penetrations of the hood may be welded so long as the weld is smooth, not creating a grease trap, and is cleanable
- Internal hood joints, seams and filter support frames, inside the hood shall be scaled or otherwise made greasetight
- Penetrations shall be sealed by devices that are listed
- Listed exhaust hoods with or without exhaust dampers shall be constructed and assembled in accordance with the listing

Recirculating hood

Canopy hood - 18 gauge - stainless steel - 2 m (6' 6") off the floor (IMC)

Backsplash Clearance

Behind the appliances, fire clearance protection must be provided either from the floor to the bottom of the hood or to noncombustible material.

Generally NFPA 96, Section 4.2.3.2 is applied for clearances behind the metal backsplash panels at the back of the appliances.

> *NFPA 96, Section 4.2.3.2: Where a clearance reduction system consisting of 0.69 mm (0.027 in.) (22-gauge) sheet metal on 25 mm (1 in.) mineral wool bats or ceramic fiber blanket reinforced with wire mesh or equivalent spaced out 25 mm (1 in.) on noncombustible spacers is provided, there shall be a minimum of 76 mm (3 in.) clearance to combustible material.*

IMC 507.9 Clearance Exceptions for Type I Hoods allow the exception that no clearance is required for gypsum board if attached to noncombustible structures, provided that it is smooth, cleanable, and non-absorbent.

Hood Clearance

Most hood manufacturers build a 3 in. rib system to the back of the hood to create the 3 inches required by code.

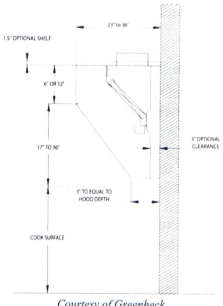

Courtesy of Greenheck.

The backside of a "wall mounted" canopy hood. The 3" spacer can be seen.

Non-Compliant Hoods

Editorial note: Because of the nature of non-compliant issues, many of the comments in this section are editorial.

Type II hoods (or systems) are only allowed over nongrease-producing appliances. Type II systems are non-compliant when used over grease-producing appliances. Type II hoods are supposed to be only fume hoods, used for the removal of dry (oven) heat, steam or odors.

This is one of the most dangerous fire situations in restaurant kitchens. Literally thousands of non-compliant systems are being used over grease-producing appliances. The ability of the Inspector to identify these systems is critical to fire safety.

Type II riveted hood

NFPA 96, Section A.3.3.34 (2) Hood Type II. Hoods designed for heat and steam removal and other nongrease applications. These hoods are not applicable to the standard.

Two categories are included in Type II Hoods:

- Condensate hoods for applications including high-moisture exhaust. Filters are generally included.

- Fume hoods for applications including only heat and fumes. Filters are optional and are not usually included.

Some jurisdictions lack codes relating to kitchen fire safety. In other areas, the codes for cooking operations are not enforced. For whatever reason, many building and fire departments allow non-compliant systems to remain. This results in thousands of unsafe exhaust systems.

Many times restaurants will install non-compliant Type II hoods over grease-producing appliances, because they are less expensive. Or, they will remodel and replace steam equipment with grease cooking equipment under a Type II hood.

There are also appliances such as conveyor pizza ovens that claim to be nongrease-producing, yet grease-producing foods can and are being cooked on them.

Some Building Codes allow for lighter weight metals to be used over cooking appliances that do not generate grease; only steam, fumes and odors. This type of hood may not have filters.

A hood that is not solidly welded

A galley hood over a charbroiler with less than 18 in. of clearance

These fume hoods and their corresponding ductwork are not required to be continuously welded, therefore cannot be considered liquidtight.

Interesting homemade hoods. These are completely inadequate to protect against fire and are totally non-compliant.

Very non-compliant aluminum hoods with mesh filters. The lightweight aluminum is folded and pop riveted in place.

Filtration

The removal of grease vapors from the cooking exhaust air begins in the hood. Filtration of grease-laden vapors is accomplished by pulling greasy air through a system of baffle filters, water mist and/or electrically charged surfaces.

Once the grease-laden air has passed through the primary filtration, other (secondary) filtration methods may be used, such as electrostatic precipitators (ESPs), active carbon filters, or Ultra-Violet Filtration.

Until recently, there was no standard test to accurately rate filters. ASHRAE's TC-5.10 Technical Committee has now successfully developed a method to rate filter extraction effectiveness. As a result ASTM has published ASTM F2519-05 *Standard Test Method for Grease Particle Capture Efficiency of Commercial Kitchen Filters and Extractors.*

Baffle filters in a canopy hood

Baffle filter
*Mesh filter – **not allowed***

Primary Filtration

Filters (grease removal devices) must conform to NFPA 96, Section 6.2, IMC 507.11.1 and UL 1046.

- No gaps are allowed between filters

- Grease filters shall be installed at an angle not less than 45 degrees from the horizontal

- Baffle filters are constructed from either aluminum or steel

- Aluminum filters are not allowed over solid fuel cooking appliances

- It is considered prudent that steel filters be used, since they withstand greater daily punishment and will not be affected by the chemicals used in the cleaning process

- Filters should be a minimum of 121.9 cm (48 in.) from the surface of a charbroiler, unless part of a listed assembly

- To remain fire-safe, filters need to be regularly removed and cleaned. The frequency of this cleaning will depend on the type and volume of cooking

- Filters must be in place during all periods of cooking

- Mesh filters are not allowed for Type I

- Must be in line and above the cooking surface

- The filters must be in place during all periods of cooking with the baffles running vertically

Filtration Types:

- Baffle filters

- Cartridge filters or removable extractors

- Dual stage filters

- Stationary baffles in water wash hoods

Illustrating the removal of a "butterfly" baffle filter

Baffle Filter

Baffle filters are now the standard in the industry and should be used in all filter-type hoods. This filter consists primarily of a series of two offsetting, corrugated, overlapping, parallel sheets of metal, attached to a standard filter frame.

Baffle filters remove grease from the air stream by means of centrifugal force. These filters possess the ability to continuously drain liquid grease as the air is pulled through them, provided that they have been correctly (vertically) installed. Many filters will have a small arrow inscribed onto one or more of the edges, indicating proper airflow direction.

There is far less buildup of grease on these filters than mesh types, because baffle filters remove grease from the air stream and drain it into a collection container. This reduces the potential fuel for a fire.

Many types of baffle filters exist; most employ stationary baffles mounted within a frame. Adjustable baffle filters are available which facilitate segmenting airflow above the cooking equipment (i.e. more air flow may be directed above higher heat and smoke generating equipment and decreased airflow above lighter output cooking equipment).

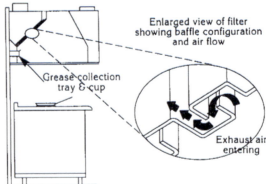

Canopy-filter type hood. Courtesy of Garland.

Solid Fuel Spark Arrester Filters

According to NFPA 96, Section 14.5.2, where a restaurant has solid cooking fuel operations with a filter type hood; it is required to install spark arrester devices.

Spark arresters are simply a coarse-grade, crisscross filter, which allow easy airflow but catch larger particles like embers that are caught in the airstream. Spark arresters, when installed in front of existing filters, will restrict almost all embers from lodging against or passing through the filter.

Numerous kitchen fires have had their origins in solid-fuel cooking operations. This occurs when glowing embers fly up from the burning solid fuels and enter a grease contaminated hood and duct system.

Important Note: One very important reason mesh filters are no longer allowed in the code is because a mesh-type filter that is plugged with grease can readily be ignited by glowing embers from solid fuel that lodge up against it.

Flame Gard Type I baffle filter
Courtesy of Component Hardware Group

An example of a spark arrester. Note the closer
"weave" of the face screen.

Cartridge Filters or Removable Extractors

Modular extractors, also known as dry cartridges or simply extractors, use a series of angular plates and baffles, similar to a water wash hood, except the baffles are contained within a removable cartridge that is removed for cleaning.

Extractors utilize a design incorporating a high velocity grease extraction plenum to remove grease-laden air. As the air from cooking enters the cartridge it is thrown into a cyclonic or centrifugal motion promoting grease extraction.

Extractors are made of stainless steel and contain full length self-draining baffles. Extractor inserts are removable for periodic cleaning. The grease collecting gutter at the bottom of the extractor housing slopes to one end, to a removable stainless steel grease collecting container. The removable doors on the face of the unit provide access to all internal components for cleaning and maintenance.

Two examples of modular extractors. Courtesy of Greenheck.

At the end of the cooking day or at periodic intervals, the inserts should be removed and washed either in a dishwasher or soaked and rinsed off.

Gaylord dry cartridge hood

Dual Stage Filters

Once the grease-laden air has passed through the primary filtration, other (secondary) filtration methods may be used. For additional information on secondary filtration and air purification used in the exhaust system, see the Air Pollution Control Units (APCU) Section of Chapter 6, Fans.

Multi-staged filters use a centrifugal type filter as the primary stage of filtration along with a packed bead bed filter as the second stage. Interception is the main filtration mechanism, which works by adsorption of grease particles as they come in contact with the packed bead bed. As these filters build up grease load their static pressure increases. Failure to regularly clean them will decrease capture.

This UL Listed assembly consists of a "Grease X-tractor" metal baffle filter, and a secondary "Grease Grabber" filter. Courtesy of Greenheck.

Non-Compliant Filters

In the late seventies, with the realization that mesh type filters posed more of a fire hazard than was acceptable, the filter industry re-thought the design and purpose of grease filters. From this research the baffle-style filter was developed.

Mesh filters are not approved for use in Type I hoods.

Mesh filters are air filters not grease filters. If used over grease-producing appliances, mesh filters will hold condensed grease inside the mesh of the filter.

When contaminated, mesh filters also constrict the airflow, resulting in an uneven and inconsistent draw across the surface of the hood.

The grease may not be removed thoroughly at the time of cleaning. This buildup provides an excellent fuel source. It can be a contributing factor for sustained combustion in the interior of a hood.

Mesh filters are reported to have caught fire and burned for some time before the staff ever knew they had a fire.

Mesh filters have a tendency to reintroduce grease back into the air stream, as it drips off the back of the filter media.

Note: If you encounter mesh filters, strongly recommend replacement.

Mesh filters used in a canopy hoods over grease-producing cooking operations

A steel mesh filter after a fire

Improper Filter Placement

One of the most common problems with baffle filters is that they will be installed incorrectly. The baffles must run vertically so the captured oils will drain off. Filters installed with the baffles running horizontally are useless.

An example of a spark arrestor. Note the filter on the left is installed incorrectly. (photo on left)

These filters are a real problem. Not only are they running the wrong way, but also there is such a gap between them that little or no grease will be captured. If there was a fire, the flames would be easily pulled through the openings. (on right)

Hood Dampers

Dampers

Requirements for dampers are found at NFPA 96, Section 5.3.4.

There are listed hood designs that include dampers in the throat of the hood just before the duct or within the hood assembly. In the case of a fire in the hood, the damper will close and prevent the fire from penetrating the duct system.

Basically, all listed hoods fall into two sub-categories in UL Standard 710: with or without dampers. Dampers are only permitted if the hood has been tested with a damper and listed as such.

Fire damper in a hood

While UL does not identify water wash hoods, they are identified in the UL Directory as "water wash hoods with fire actuated dampers."

Note: Having a damper in a hood whether it is a water wash hood or otherwise does <u>not</u> fulfill the requirements of UL 300.

- Fire-actuated dampers are required in the supply air plenum at each point where a supply air duct inlet or a supply air outlet penetrates the continuously welded shell of the assembly

- The actuation device shall have a maximum temperature rating of 141°C (286°F)

Fusible Link Damper

The fusible links melt at 149°C (300°F). Any one link will release the damper allowing it to close by gravity and/or springs, providing a fire barrier.

Automatic Damper

An electric thermostat senses heat and activates the damper mechanism. A manual reset is provided. In a fire condition, the fan motor shuts off and the damper automatically closes, providing a fire barrier.

Recently, design standards have changed and now require fire-extinguishing systems to cover the duct area directly above the hood. Many times these requirements are not harmonious with dampers in the hood, as the piping for a fire-extinguishing system will block the damper from closing. A variety of new designs of fire damper assemblies and fire-extinguishing systems are now appearing on the market.

The inspector needs to ensure that dampers and fire-extinguishing components used will work compatibly. This will require advance knowledge of the plans for both the type of hood and extinguishing systems. Systems installers should prove to the Inspector that all systems work in a coordinated manner.

Damper Fusible Link Type: Fusible links are rated to activate at 182°C (360°F) in the exhaust duct and 141°C (286°F) in the supply duct. When this temperature is exceeded, the fusible link melts allowing the fire damper to fall closed. This linkage should be inspected and the fusible links replaced annually. Fusible links in the exhaust duct collar are readily accessible by removing the baffle filters or grease extractor. An access plate is provided for access into (supply) duct collar for all models.

Electro-Mechanical Type: These switches close electrically at temperatures above 149°C (300°F) and activate a solenoid, which releases the damper, and energizes a relay that activates the plenum auto wash/fire-extinguishing spray and deactivates the fan. In the event of a loss of power, the damper assembly also contains a fusible link, set at 182°C (360°F).

In all cases where there are dampers present in the system, it is imperative that they be kept clean and free of any blockage. In a fire situation they can be rendered useless if they cannot seal properly because of grease buildup.

Access above Dampered Hoods

Access is required in the duct immediately above any hood with a damper, especially water wash types. This is because many of these damper designs block access into the lower area of the duct for cleaning and inspection. NFPA 96, Section 7.3.4 states this access be within 457.2 mm (18 in.) or less of the hood. Failure to provide access will render the lower section of the duct inaccessible.[5]

Additionally, there has to be a rated fire door providing access through the sub-ceiling and/or walls to get to any openings, detector links and/or fire dampers within the ducts.

Non-Compliant Dampers

In most cases dampers in any part of an exhaust system is a bad idea, unless the dampers are tended to on a regular basis (which rarely happens). Grease can build up on the mechanisms and fusible links to compromise the purpose of the damper. Either it will not activate or, because of grease buildup in the area, will not be able to create a fire proof seal between the hood and the rest of the system.

> *NFPA 96, Section 9.1.1: Dampers shall not be installed in exhaust ducts or exhaust duct systems.*
>
> *9.1.2 Where specifically listed for such use or where required as part of a listed device or system, dampers in exhaust ducts or exhaust duct systems shall be permitted.*

Damper inside a duct that is completely frozen from grease buildup

---

[5] Also see IMC 507.8.

A spring-loaded damper just before a fan. The link and damperhave not been tested in years.

Back draft baffle dampers allowed in some States. These plug with grease and jam up easily. They are not allowed in NFPA 96.

Water Wash Type Hoods

Some of the manufacturers of these systems are:

- Gaylord Industries
- Quest (CleanAir)
- Ventmaster
- AVTEC

- Southern Engineering Company
- Spring Air Systems
- Crown Simplex
- Greenheck

Crown Simplex hood. On the right, the panels have been removed.

Water Wash Hoods

Water wash hoods utilize a system of removable cartridges or baffles and metal angles or fixed angles to pull the grease out of the air. As the grease and dirt particles from the air stream pass through the angles at high speed, the grease is thrown out of the air stream by centrifugal force. The extracted grease is collected in the lower troughs of the hood and remains out of the air stream until removed by a daily wash cycle.

The wash cycle can be operated manually or programmed for automatic self-washing during certain times of the day and for specific durations of time. Most models allow for adjustment of the flow rate for the detergent.

The wash controls, pumps, plumbing assemblies, timer, cycle controls, and detergent injectors are usually housed within a control cabinet, or panel located inside the kitchen. Information on the model and mechanical servicing that has taken place will be located there as well.

Water wash assemblies must be provided with inspection covers or doors so the interior of the ventilator can periodically be checked for grease accumulation.

If the wash function is not working properly, these systems will accumulate dangerously large amounts of grease in the trough. This is serious because potential flare-ups on the cooking equipment can ignite this grease buildup.

Note: Many water wash hoods do not receive regular mechanical servicing. Over heavy grease producing cooking, these systems may not function as designed.

Automatic Washing

By pushing the "start wash" button on the command center (or as programmed, if equipped with optional time clock) the water wash system is activated, and the exhaust fan stopped. Hot water and detergent is then sprayed into the ventilator.

A water/detergent mixture is sprayed from a series of nozzles for a pre-set time period to remove accumulated grease and grime, which flows out through the drain. At the end of the wash cycle, the water automatically shuts off.

Hot water should be between 130° and 180° (54°C and 82°C) and pressure must be to the manufacturer's specifications. The duration of the wash down cycle is adjustable and will vary depending on the length of cooking cycle, type of cooking equipment used, concentration of detergent, water pressure and temperature, among other considerations.

A Quest water wash hood during "wash" cycle

A VentMaster water wash hood that has removable covers (which have been removed)

A cut away of a Greenheck water wash hood

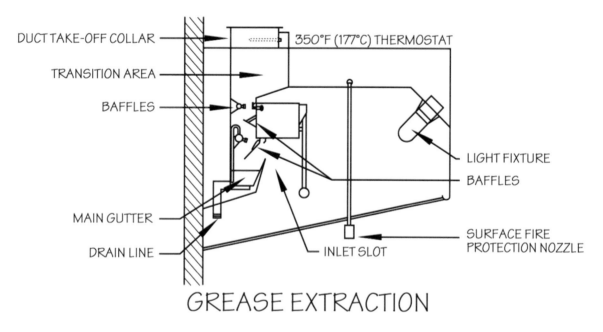

DUCT TAKE-OFF COLLAR
350°F (177°C) THERMOSTAT
TRANSITION AREA
BAFFLES
LIGHT FIXTURE
BAFFLES
MAIN GUTTER
SURFACE FIRE PROTECTION NOZZLE
DRAIN LINE
INLET SLOT

GREASE EXTRACTION

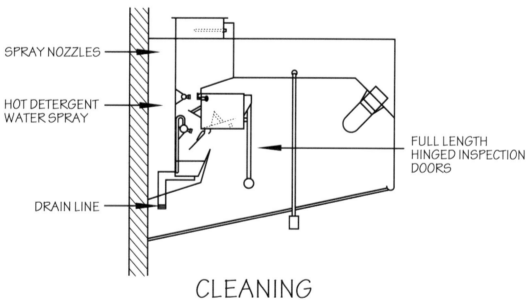

SPRAY NOZZLES
HOT DETERGENT WATER SPRAY
FULL LENGTH HINGED INSPECTION DOORS
DRAIN LINE

CLEANING

Courtesy of Gaylord Industries

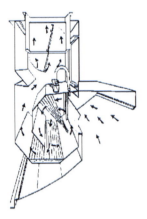

A cross section of an older VentMaster water wash system

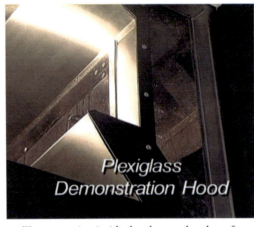

Water spraying inside the plenum chamber of a Greenheck water wash hood

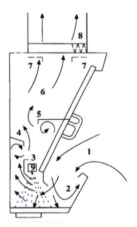

Airflow in Cyclo Maze cold water mist unit

Cold Water Mist (optional)

To aid in extracting particulates from the exhausted air, a continuous water mist option is available. This is especially useful when charbroilers, solid fuel equipment or woks are involved. Cold-water mist is a fine spray within the plenum area that runs whenever the fans are on. This complements the baffle system but does not replace the wash down feature.

Inspectors should confirm that the mist system is functioning properly.

Dampers in Water Wash Hoods

If the surface fire-extinguishing system fails to extinguish the fire, the water wash hood dampering system then acts as a backup to protect the hood interior and prevent the fire from extending into the ductwork.

Editorial Comment: One of the major benefits of a listed water wash type hood is that it is designed to offer a degree of protection in case of a fire. However, if all components of the system are not mechanically maintained these systems are prone to malfunction, particularly the dampers and wash system. See NFPA 96, Sections 11.2 and 11.3.

A service frequency of 6 months is required for listed hoods with fire-actuated water systems, mechanical or electrical detectors, actuators, and fire-actuated dampers. These hoods should be checked according to the manufacturers listed procedures and specific inspection requirements of applicable NFPA 96 Standards. See NFPA 11.2.1

Pull levers of water wash hood dampers (circled in bottom picture)

Fire-Extinguishing in Water Wash Hoods

Water wash hoods are designed to both control and contain fire. The fire-extinguishing system is always the first line of defense. If the fire-extinguishing system fails to control the fire, the water wash hood damper closes and the water system is activated. The intent is to limit the fire spread within the hood. This approach relies heavily on the proper mechanical function of the hood.

Note: NFPA 96 also requires a fire-extinguishing system in water wash hoods.

Most manufacturers provide automatic and manual fire-cycle activators (the most common being Fenwal), by way of thermostats in the duct and/or a manual fire pull-station, generally installed near the kitchen exit. These controls initiate the dampers (internal fire containment) system. If the thermostat initiates the fire cycle, the water sprays come on, the damper closes and the fan shuts down.

Note to Inspectors: Although the manufacturer's claim that these hoods have some "fire protection" value, in the field a large number of these hoods are not receiving proper mechanical maintenance to ensure the wash cycle and dampers will function as designed in a fire. Regular maintenance is required. Check the control panel for dates of last service.

Water Wash Hoods and Fire-Extinguishing Systems

Water wash hoods are designed to activate their water wash and damper systems during a fire situation. When functioning properly this action will assist in stopping the fire from getting beyond the hood and suppressing the fire in the plenum area of the hood.

Editorial Note: The following is only the opinion of the author of this publication. NFPA 96, Section 10.2 seems contradictory. Individual research and comments should be obtained from the water wash hood and fire-extinguishing system manufacturers.

> *NFPA 96, Section 10.2.8.1: Grease removal devices, hood exhaust plenums, and exhaust ducts requiring protection in accordance with 10.1.1 shall be permitted to be protected by a listed fixed baffle hood containing a constant or fire-actuated water-wash system that is listed in compliance with ANSI/UL 300 or other equivalent standards and shall be installed in accordance with the requirements of their listing.*

Editorial Note: It is the authors understanding, at the time of this publication, there is <u>no such product</u> on the market as "*…a listed fixed baffle hood containing a constant or fire-actuated water-wash system that is listed in compliance with ANSI/UL 300 or other equivalent standard…*" Therefore, the requirements of NFPA 96, Section 10.2.8.2 are necessary to comply with UL 300 and NFPA 96.

> *NFPA 96, Section 10.2.8.2: Each such area not provided with a listed water wash extinguishing system shall be provided with a fire-extinguishing system listed for the purpose.*

This does not then excuse the water wash hood from performing the task it was designed for; controlling fire in the plenum area of the hood.

> *NFPA 96, Section 10.2.8.5: The water wash in a fixed baffle hood, specifically listed to extinguish a fire, shall be activated by the cooking equipment extinguishing system.*

Again, there are no "specifically listed" water wash systems for extinguishing a fire.

> *NFPA 96, Section 10.2.8.6: A water-wash system, approved to be used for protection of the grease removal device(s), hood exhaust plenum(s), exhaust duct(s), or combination thereof shall include instruction and appropriate electrical interface for simultaneous activation of the water-wash system from an automatic fire-extinguishing system, where the automatic fire-extinguishing system is used for cooking equipment protection only.*

An inspector should ask to see these instructions on the premise.

> *NFPA 96, Section 10.2.8.7: Where the fire-extinguishing system provides protection for the cooking equipment, hood, and duct, activation of the water wash shall not be required.*

However, NFPA 96, Section 10.2.8.7 states that if there is a fire-extinguishing system protecting the hood and duct, then the water wash system <u>does not need to activate.</u> This is a contradiction from the purpose for having a water wash system.

Looking down into the trough of an older water wash hood. Arrows are pointing to the wash nozzles. This picture was taken just after the hood was manually cleaned.

Non-Compliant Water Wash Hoods

As stated earlier in this manual, water wash hoods in general suffer from lack of mechanical maintenance. These units can only function properly if they are professionally maintained. The interior of most systems is not easily visible for inspection by the kitchen staff. Ensure that there is a mechanical maintenance contract in place. This does not mean a cleaning or fire-extinguishing system contract. They are totally different.

Grease buildup on removable water wash cartridges. Both components were serving over charbroilers.

An open door of a Gaylord water wash. The system had not been mechanically serviced for years.

Looking down from an access panel in the duct into the top section of a water wash hood that was not operating properly.

Inspecting the trough of two water wash hoods

Air Pollution Control Units (APCU)

An Air Pollution Control Unit is a metal compartment in the airstream of the exhaust system. The compartment contains a series of filters that purify and deodorize the contaminated air. These units are normally located on the roof or in a mechanical room.

Most APCU's consist of several components: a filter section, an odor-reducing section, and an exhaust section. An optional energy reclamation section is also available.

Some models utilize electrostatic precipitation (ESP) to remove the smoke particles and may include optional odor control.

As energy and construction costs have escalated, the use of air pollution control units have increased, especially in northern climates. These air pollution control units provide the means by which the hot, grease-laden air that is drawn off from the cooking process is filtered and refined to the point where it can (in some jurisdictions) be reintroduced into the living space of the building.

For these systems to work properly a number of technologies must work together in an efficient and coordinated manner.

If a fire takes place and the hood dampers and fire-extinguishing system do not function properly, the fire could easily reach the grease-saturated filters of these units. The subsequent smoke could be pumped directly into the occupied (living) space of the building. Therefore, it is critical that these units be maintained properly.

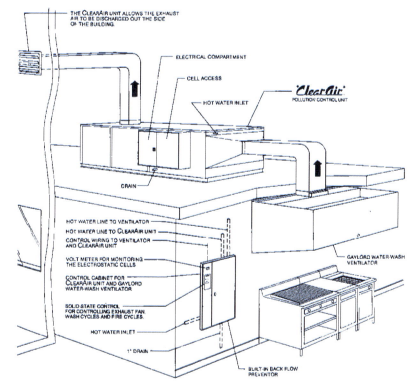

Diagram of Gaylord air pollution control system

Important Note:

Using an air pollution control unit without the filters creates little more than a forced air exhaust or recirculating system. Failure to maintain these systems as listed can result in serious fire and health hazards.

A "Smog Hogg"

Additionally, because of the varied types and styles of cooking and grease loads it is very important to ensure that all the components of the exhaust system are designed and coordinated according to the type of application they will be used over. Any changes to the cooking application or types of appliances used could seriously alter the efficiency of the overall filtration system.

Monitor Control Panels

All APCU systems should be integrated with their corresponding manufacturers' water wash hoods. The installer will then coordinate all the controls of the hood washing system with the APCU. Only factory trained service technicians should work on these systems.

Parts of an Air Pollution Control Unit

The mechanical components of an air pollution control unit are:

- Ducting
- Fire Damper
- Filtration Section
- Odor Removal Section

- Exhaust Fan Section
- Control Panel
- Discharge

Examples of a Paper Pre-filter, Bag Filter and HEPA Filter

Air pollution control units shall be installed in accordance with NFPA 96, Section 9.3 Other Equipment:

- Any device installed in the duct (airstream of grease vapors) shall be specifically approved for such use

- The ductwork at the exhaust end of the device must stand up to NFPA 96 standards for commercial kitchen duct systems

- All secondary filtration or air pollution systems must be protected with an approved automatic fire-extinguishing system, which protects both the component sections of the unit and the internal downstream ductwork.

- If the APCU recirculates air back into the occupied space of the building, the requirements of NFPA 96, Chapter 13 shall apply

- All APCUs and any other secondary filtration system in the ductwork should be listed for the use. The unit shall be operated, inspected and maintained in accordance with the manufacturer's listing.[6]

---

[6] For further information on Recirculating Systems, see NFPA 96, Chapter 13.

Chapter Five – Fire-Extinguishing Systems

A suppression distribution system that is preventing the grease filter from being installed

Fire-Extinguishing Systems

Introduction

This chapter addresses fire protection principles and requirements for commercial cooking appliances and exhaust system fire-extinguishing equipment including:

- Pre-Engineered Fixed Pipe Fire-Extinguishing Systems (Primary Protection)

- Water Sprinkler Systems

- Portable Fire Extinguishers (Secondary Protection)

Fire-extinguishing system distribution nozzles and detection links

Extinguishing a fire in a commercial kitchen is no simple matter. Fires will generally involve very hot oils, as well as electricity, gas and ordinary combustibles such as paper, wood and cloth. Prior to the 1960's, portable and manually controlled CO2 systems were used to extinguish fires.

In the early 1960's, the first dry chemical fixed pipe extinguishers were developed. Dry chemical powder was generally a sodium bicarbonate base.

The major drawback to dry chemical agents is that it does not adequately blanket and cool down the burning oils and other surfaces of appliances. For this reason in the early 1980's new wet chemical suppressants were developed to provide superior and cleaner fire protection.[1] Dry chemical systems are no longer allowed, as they are not compliant with UL 300 or NFPA 96 Standards.

In 2002, specially listed water sprinkler systems, as Listed in UL199E, was employed for protection of this hazard. These systems have automatic fire detector bulbs built into the nozzle head; but no manual pull exists.

General Standards

UL - 300 and ULC/ORD - 1254.6

As of 1994 both Underwriters Laboratories and Underwriters Laboratories of Canada re-defined the listing requirements and test protocols for "Wet Chemical" extinguishing agents. These changes came about as a direct result of changing cooking styles and improved energy-efficient cooking equipment.

Oils are composed of "triglycerides," which consist of three long fatty acids chains attached to a glycerine backbone. As they deteriorate from heating, the triglycerides come apart, releasing free fatty acids into the oil.

In the past few years, restaurants have changed cooking oil from animal fats, which contain high levels of free fatty acids, to vegetable oils, which contain significantly lower levels of free fatty acids.

Extinguishing agents are used to saponify (which means turn into soap) and form a blanket of foam, when they react with the free fatty acids. However, with lower levels of fatty acids, saponification was decreased; therefore, changes were required in the chemical make-up of the wet chemical extinguishing agent.

The new UL 300 and ULC/ORD 1254.6 1995 testing parameters are a more accurate reflection of "real world" situations compared to previous wet chemical testing parameters. In laymen's terms, "the wet just got wetter." The change in the cooking medium from animal fats to vegetable oils also resulted in higher autoignition temperatures of the cooking oil compared to animal fats. The autoignition temperature of most vegetable oils is approximately 363 ºC (685 ºF), which is as much as 57 ºC (135 ºF) higher than the autoignition temperatures of animal fat.

---

[1] The first wet chemical system was developed in 1964 by Range Guard owned (at the time) by Automatic Sprinkler Corporation, but it took years before wet chemical came on the market.

The higher autoignition temperatures of the cooking oil and a change to more energy-efficient cooking equipment, allowed the oil to retain heat for a longer period of time.[2]

Clean vegetable oil fires are harder to extinguish due to the higher initial heat; because the major portion of wet chemical systems is water, more agent needs to be applied before the fire can be knocked down. That is the reason UL300 wet systems require more wet agent than pre UL300. The pre UL300 test protocol allowed for the use of mock appliances, immediate gas shut off at the first sign of flame, one minute pre-burn before system actuation and no reflash for 5 minutes. The UL300 test protocol is much more stringent; it requires real functional appliances, two minute pre-burn with fuel on before system actuation and no reflash for 20 minutes (fryers were found to reflash 8 to 10 minutes after initial knockdown due to heat retention and movement or breakdown of saponified layer above oil on the pre UL300 applications).

For these reasons, only wet chemical systems are approved for cooking equipment protection under the revised test protocol. Most areas require that wet chemical extinguishing systems be up to UL 300 or ULC/ORD 1254.6 1995 listing. It must be noted that there are still a few jurisdictions that continue to allow pre-UL 300 wet chemical systems to remain in use.

NFPA 96 and 17A Fire-Extinguishing System Requirements

In commercial cooking facilities, fixed fire-extinguishing systems are the primary means of fire control. NFPA 96, Chapter 10 requires fire-extinguishing equipment for the protection of hoods, exhaust plenums, exhaust duct systems, and grease removal devices. Cooking equipment that produces grease-laden vapors and could be a source of ignition of grease in the exhaust system is also required to be protected by a fire-extinguishing system.

Additional NFPA 96, Chapter 10 requirements:

- Fire-extinguishing systems shall comply with UL 300

- Any appliances and exhaust components that are not addressed in UL 300 or other equivalent test standards, shall be protected with an automatic fire-extinguishing system(s) in accordance with the applicable NFPA standards, local codes, and approved by the AHJ

- Automatic fire-extinguishing equipment provided in listed recirculating systems must comply with UL 197, Standard for Commercial Electric Cooking Appliances

- Systems in single hazard areas shall be arranged for simultaneous operation upon activation of any of the systems

- All sources of fuel or electric power for cooking equipment shall be automatically shut off

- Readily accessible means of manual activation shall be in a path of egress

- An audible or visual alarm shall be provided to show activation of a fire-extinguishing system

- In an occupancy provided with a fire alarm system, the fire alarm system shall activate at the same time as the cooking equipment fire-extinguishing system

NFPA 96 and 17A requires that fire protection systems be installed and maintenance manuals be consulted in accordance with ANSI/UL 300 or other equivalent standards, and applicable NFPA standards. See NFPA 10.2.3*

In addition to these requirements for fixed pipe fire-extinguishing systems, NFPA 96 also requires portable fire extinguishers listed for such use.[3]

Exhaust Fan Operation

The operation of the fan depends on the type of exhaust system installed in the kitchen. With unlisted hoods, generally fans are required to remain in operation; those over listed hoods with dampers, generally shut off. Fan shut off is covered at NFPA 96, Section 8.2.3.

---

[2] Lake, James D, Section 11, Chapter 4 Chemical Extinguishing Agents and Application Systems, NFPA Fire Protection Handbook 19th Edition.

[3] See the Portable Fire Extinguisher Section in this chapter.

- The exhaust fans shall continue to operate after the extinguishing system has been activated unless fan shutdown is required by a listed component of the ventilation system or the extinguishing system

- If shut off at the time of fire-extinguishing activation, the exhaust fan is not required to restart

- Makeup air supplied through the hood, must shut off when the exhaust system's fire-extinguishing system discharges

- When its fire-extinguishing system discharges, makeup air supplied internally to a hood shall be shut off.

Power Shut Down

NFPA 96, Section 10.4 deals with power shut down of appliances under fire situations:

- Upon activation of any fire-extinguishing system, all gas appliances and all others sources of fuel and power that produce heat on appliances are required to automatically shut off

- Shutoff devices shall require manual reset

Water Wash Hoods and Fire-Extinguishing Systems

Editorial Note: It is the authors understanding, at the time of this publication, there is <u>no such product</u> on the market as *"...a listed fixed baffle hood containing a constant or fire-actuated water-wash system that is listed in compliance with ANSI/UL 300 or other equivalent standard..."* Therefore, the requirements of NFPA 96, Section 10 are necessary to comply with UL 300 and NFPA 96.

An older unmaintained water wash hood after a fire

Locations That Require Protection

Hazards and equipment that can be protected using wet chemical extinguishing systems include the following:[4]

- Restaurant, commercial and institutional hoods

- Plenums, ducts, and filters with their associated cooking appliances

- Special grease removal devices

- Odor control devices

- Energy recovery devices installed in the exhaust system

The following is a list of cooking appliances that <u>require</u> wet chemical extinguishing systems:

- Deep-fat fryers (including woks)

- Griddles and range tops

- Tilting skillets and braising pans (now considered to be deep-fat fryers)

- Upright broilers and back-shelf or "salamander" broilers

- Electric or gas radiant element broilers

- Lava or synthetic rock "char-rock" broilers

- Chain broilers

- Charcoal and Mesquite-wood broilers

- All appliances as required by the AHJ

- Any appliance that produces a grease-laden vapor

An example of a "vapor only" Type II exhaust hood over a convection oven

---

[4] See NFPA 17A, Section 5.1.2.

The following appliances <u>may</u> not require fire protection but still need ventilation:

- Totally enclosed ovens

- Steam appliances

- Bun warmer appliances which do not produce enough heat to broil meats

- Industrial sized coffee urns

Wet Chemical Fire-Extinguishing Systems

There are several manufacturers of fire-extinguishing systems. These systems consist of the manufacturer's hardware and additional installation components. The primary components consist of agent storage cylinders, discharge valves, detection components, piping, and agent distribution nozzles.

Properly capped fire-extinguishing nozzles in front of filters with spark arresters

The manufacturer prepares a design guide that is approved by UL. This design depicts the requirements and considerations that must be applied to various appliance, hood and duct configurations. This method is based on engineering and that has been tested by UL. This allows the installation distributor to design systems in the field in accordance with the design guides, and be assured that they will meet the requirements of UL 300. On this basis the systems are called "Pre-engineered."

Most of the mechanical components of fixed wet and dry chemical systems are similar.

Wet chemical fire-extinguishing agent, pre-engineered extinguishing systems are listed for the protection of commercial cooking appliances and exhaust systems under UL 300, *Standard for Fire Testing of Fire Extinguishing Systems for Protection of Restaurant Cooking Areas* (or other equivalent standards) and that the systems be installed in accordance with the terms of the listing. This UL standard addresses wet chemical systems, which are now the most prevalent types used for this special hazard protection.

The agents are proprietary mixtures of potassium carbonate, potassium acetate, potassium citrate, or a combination in water with other additives to form an alkaline suppressant. The wet chemical agents are stored in containers up to 34 L (9 gal.) in capacity, and most systems utilize nitrogen or carbon dioxide in pressurized cartridges or the chemical cylinders themselves to expel the agent through the distribution piping. When the wet chemical agents are discharged on a grease fire, the fire is extinguished by a combination of smothering and cooling.

Some wet chemical systems are arranged with a connection to a domestic water supply. After discharge of the wet chemical, water is discharged through the nozzles providing additional cooling.

Installation of Fire-Extinguishers

NFPA 17A, Section 6.1* Specifications (2002 Edition). Specifications for wet chemical fire-extinguishing systems shall be drawn up with care under the supervision of a trained person and with the advice of the authority having jurisdiction.

6.2* Review and Certification. Design and installation of systems shall be performed only by persons properly trained and qualified to design and/or install the specific system being provided.

The installer shall provide certification to the authority having jurisdiction that the installation is in complete agreement with the terms of the listing and the manufacturer's instructions and/or approved design.

When a fire-extinguishing system is installed, the AHJ and the insurance company usually require an Acceptance Test. This test confirms that the system is operational. The installer should provide the restaurant with documentation of the installation and upkeep requirements and the results of the test. The installer may also provide copies to the Building and/or Fire Department.

- Only persons properly trained and qualified are to install the specific system being provided

- Installer shall provide certification to the AHJ that the installation is in accordance with the listing, manufacturer's instructions and/or approved design

- No abandoned pipe or conduit from previous extinguisher systems shall remain in the hood or exhaust system

- All penetrations and holes from previously installed piping shall be sealed with listed or equivalent liquidtight devices

- If there are changes to the cooking line or other modifications to the fire hazard, the fire-extinguishing system is required to be re-evaluated by qualified persons

Fire-Extinguishing System Owner's Responsibilities

NFPA 17A provides a list of responsibilities for the owner of the fire-extinguishing system. The following points from that Standard should be reviewed during an interview with the owner.[5]

Inspections that should be conducted on a monthly basis:

- Fire-extinguishing system (nozzles) are in proper locations

- Manual pulls are not obstructed

- Tamper indicators and seals on the control head are intact

- Maintenance tag is in place

- No obvious physical damage or condition exists that might prevent operation

- Pressure gauges are in operable range

- Nozzle blowoff caps are intact and undamaged

Attitude of most management

- Hood, duct, and protected cooking appliances have not been replaced, modified, or relocated

- Other than for normal cleaning and maintenance the appliances requiring protection shall not be moved, modified, or rearranged without prior reevaluation of the fire-extinguishing system unless other-wise allowed by the fire-extinguishing system design

- An approved method shall be provided that will ensure that the appliance is returned to an approved design location

- Staff knows how to operate the system correctly

NFPA 96, Sections 11 and 12 further expand on responsibilities of the restaurant management.[6]

NFPA 96, Section 11.1.4: Instructions for manually operating the fire-extinguishing system shall be posted conspicuously in the kitchen and shall be reviewed with employees by the management.

11.1.6 Cooking equipment shall not be operated while its fire-extinguishing system or exhaust system is nonoperational or impaired.

---

[5] See NFPA 17A, Section 7.2, Owner's Inspection.

[6] For further details see Key Changes in Chapter 2, Codes.

How Fixed Pipe Fire-Extinguishing Works

Dry or wet chemical automatic fire-extinguishing systems will consist of a release mechanism, agent tank, piping to direct chemical agents, an electric or cable detection system encased in tubing, fusible links, and fuel shutdown equipment.

These systems are designed to apply chemical (wet or dry) fire-extinguishing agents or water (fog) into the hood and ductwork and onto the cooking surface.

All wet or dry chemical fire-extinguishing systems must have fire detectors and agent discharge nozzles located in the duct collar, in the hood behind the filters, and positioned to cover cooking appliances requiring protection.

A small fire on one cooking appliance can quickly spread. Flames are then drawn up into the hood and duct, igniting the accumulated grease within.

When a fire starts in these enclosed areas, one or more of the fire-extinguishing fusible links, or an electric thermoswitch fire detector, activates. The link separates, releasing the tension in the cable connected to the system control head, opening the cylinder valve.

Or the thermoswitch closes completing an electrical circuit.

The fire-extinguishing agent is propelled by gas pressure through the agent distribution system and is discharged through all nozzles simultaneously. This puts agent directly onto the fire as well as applying agent to the areas where the fire can spread.

When the chemical agent comes in contact with hot or burning grease, it forms synthetic foam, which should cover the grease and smother the fire. The foam barrier extinguishes the fire by separating the fuel from the oxygen. Water vaporization and formation of foam on the surface also cools the fuel and the appliances, minimizing the danger of the fire re-flashing.

For demonstration purposes we melted this link and activated the extinguishing system

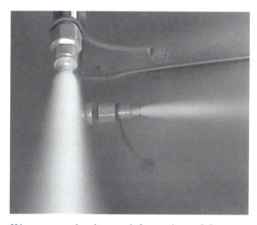

Upon actuation, the fuel source to the cooking appliances is automatically shut off, as required by NFPA 96. All sources of electrical power under the hood must shut down. This will allow the appliances to cool down, also reducing the possibility of a reflash of the fire.

Note: The staff can activate the system manually. In a fire situation, detectors will not respond as quickly if heavily coated with grease.

Dry Chemical and Cooking Oil Fires

Dry chemicals when applied to grease or cooking oils (as in a fryer or on top of a griddle) mix with the grease and create a foamy soap (saponify). This foam layer cuts off the oxygen leg of the traditional fire triangle. In this case saponified powder actually suffocates the fire. Dry chemical does not work well on grease fires, particularly on the vegetable oils now used in fryers (compared to the animal fat used before). Additionally, it is important to note that this saponified powder acts as an insulator, therefore no cooling effect occurs. Disturbing this layer results in fire reflash (thus the reason for wet application which does cool the fuel to below flash point).

Example of a fire that was not contained by faulty dry chemical systems

Wet Chemical Extinguishing Components

All fire-extinguishing parts should be indicated as Factory Authorized and/or UL/ULC listed. There are UL listed parts for use with multiple system manufacturers. While not factory approved they have been tested and listed by UL.

Mechanical or Electrical Systems

The fire-extinguishing system can be operated either mechanically or electrically.

The mechanical system consists of a valve system that is mechanically operated by a spring mechanism. The mechanism is held in a standby mode by a system of cables that are held in tension by fusible link heat detectors. When the temperature increases, a fusible link melts and releases the tension on the cable allowing the activation of the cylinder valves. No outside power is required to operate the mechanical systems.

The electrical system uses a valve system that is electrically operated by a solenoid to activate a spring mechanism to open the valve. Heat detectors that switch the power to the solenoid control the supply of current. When the temperature increases the thermoswitch electrical contacts close switching power to operate the solenoid.

Note: "System" could mean only the detection or distribution system of the fire-extinguishing system.

Detection System

Wet chemical systems utilize the following types of detector units:

- Fusible links
- Quartzoid bulb
- Electric

Detection devices must be installed in the proper locations in accordance with the fire-extinguishing system manufacturer's instructions. The devices are placed above each appliance or group of appliances protected by a discharge nozzle (UL 300 states each protected appliance shall have its own detector and its own nozzle or nozzles).

Fusible Ansul "scissor" link

Detection is also required at the duct entrance in a hood, or above electronic precipitators (if provided).

Note: In a fire situation, detectors will not respond as quickly when heavily coated with grease.

Fusible Links

See NFPA 11.2 for inspection of fire-extinguisher systems

One of the most critical parts of a fire-extinguishing system is the fusible link.

> *NFPA 96, Section 11.2.4*: Fusible links of the metal alloy type and automatic sprinklers of the metal alloy type shall be replaced at least semiannually except as permitted by 11.2.6 and 11.2.7.*
>
> *11.2.5: The year of manufacture and the date of installation of the fusible links shall be marked on the system inspection tag.*
>
> *11.2.5.1 The tag shall be signed or initialed by the installer.*
>
> *11.2.5.2 The fusible links shall be destroyed when removed.*

Example of a fusible link.
The link is at the bottom of the assembly.

Fusible links are attached to the middle of a bracket and are designed to melt and separate at temperatures between 74° to 260°C (165° to 500°F) with many ratings in between. These links must be replaced semi annually or more frequently, according to manufacturer's instructions.

There is a stamped date on the link, however these devices have unlimited shelf life. The date stamped on the link should be reported on the fire-extinguishing system inspection tag. The date of the change should also be noted. The intent of the stamped date is to ensure the link in use is changed at least once a year.[7]

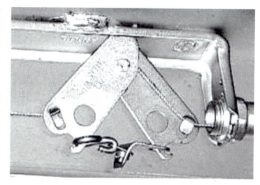

Another fusible link

Note: Many fusible links are made by outside companies; a stamp on the link indicates manufacturers approval. For example an "A" indicates Ansul or a "K" (with a circle around it) indicates Kidde. The very same link with no stamped symbol may cost 50% less, but is not approved in some jurisdictions.

If the link does not bear the manufacturer's symbol, the system manufacturer may try to disavow any responsibility for the link (and possibly the entire system's) performance.

Quartzoid Bulbs

The quartzoid bulb type detector contains a thin, liquid filled bulb in which the liquid expands from the heat and ruptures the bulb at a fixed temperature, releasing the detection cable.

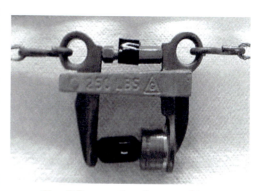

Two different styles of quartzoid links

Quartzoid type links are required to be removed, cleaned, and inspected at each servicing of system. The normal procedure is to wash with warm soapy water and a soft brush. No harsh cleansers or caustics are permitted in the cleaning process. If all grease and contamination cannot be removed the link must be replaced.

The quartzoid bulb link must be changed after twenty five years.

Electric Detectors

Electrically activated detectors contain two strips of metal that expand with heat, making or breaking contact and activating an electrical switch, which starts the flow of agent.

Note: Regardless of the type of detection device, proper fire-extinguishing system operation is dependant on the prompt response of the link or release device. Links and sensors must be of the proper rating and installed in locations that permit a prompt response to abnormal (fire plume) temperatures. Further, all detection devices must be inspected and cleaned (if coated with grease, they can have a slower response than designed).[8]

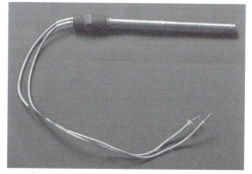

Example of a Fenwal fixed temperature electrical detector

---

[7] See NFPA 17A, Annex 7.3.3.

[8] Demers, David P., Section 12, Chapter 9 Ventilation of Commercial Cooking Operations, NFPA Fire Protection Handbook 19, pp. 12-159, 12-160.

Pulleys and Cables

The corner pulley can be used in both low and high temperature environments. The pulley contains steel ball bearings and the body is cast aluminum. 0.2 cm (1/16 in.) diameter stainless steel 7x7 strand cable must be used for the detection line. It is installed in 1.3 cm (0.5 in.) electric metallic tubing pipe (EMT).

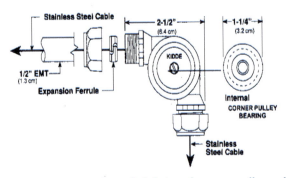

An exploded view of a corner pulley and a picture of the complete piece

Electrical Metallic Tubing (EMT)

Over high volume cooking, especially solid fuel and wok cooking, the EMT piping can become clogged with grease residue. As this residue compacts and hardens from time and heat, it will bind the pull cable. If a fire takes place, this grease blockage can stop or delay the activation of the system.

During a service inspection the EMT piping (the piping that contains the cable) must be checked.

If the piping is clogged with grease, it must be replaced. This is the responsibility of the fire-extinguishing service company. This piping cannot be properly cleaned while in place.

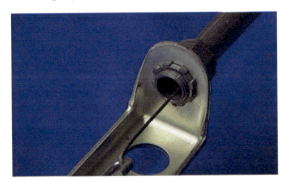

EMT piping with the cable going into it. This opening can become plugged with grease and jam the cable.

Hood and Duct Penetrations

Penetrations in the hood and duct are required to allow for the installation of fire-extinguishing system detectors and agent distribution piping and other monitoring devices. These penetrations, if not properly sealed, provide holes that grease and fire can escape from. NFPA 96, Section 5.1.11, 5.1.12 and 7.5 provides very specific requirements for these penetrations. All must be sealed with a UL listed (or equivalent) sealing device and installed according to the manufacturers listing instructions.[9]

---

[9] See UL 1978, Standard for Safety for Grease Ducts. Also see NFPA 96, Sections 7.5.2.3, 7.5.3, and 7.5.4.

Mechanical Control Heads

The melting of the fusible link releases tension in the cable allowing the control head to activate. A spring-loaded plunger depresses the cylinder valve discharging the extinguishing agent through the nozzles and onto the fire.

The control head is also equipped with a remote manual release handle.

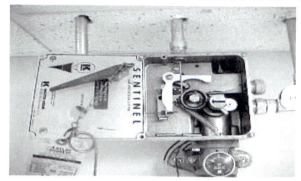

Control panel of the fire-extinguishing system with the cover removed

Remote Manual Pull Stations

A remote manual pull station is required to manually activate the release assembly.

Because fusible links sometimes fail, and because manual activation may be more efficient, a properly designed fire-extinguishing system must include a remote manual pull station mounted at a point of egress (kitchen exit) and positioned at a height of 106.7 to 121.9 cm (42 to 48 in.) above the floor.

See NFPA 96, Section 10.5 for requirements of manual activation

It should be clearly labeled and in a readily accessible location. Employees should be trained in its use.

Manual pull station

Examples of gas shut offs for fire-extinguishing systems

Mechanical and Electrical Gas Shutoff Valves

Mechanical and electrical gas valves are designed to disconnect the energy supply upon actuation of the fire-extinguishing system. Valves should be rated for natural and LP gas. Electric valves are held open by an energized solenoid and must have a reset device. Mechanical valves are held open by a cable under tension.[10]

Both styles should be listed by a recognized testing agency.

All fire-extinguishing systems use similar shut-off valves. All sources of gas or electrical power under the hood must shut down.

System Annunciation

Generally speaking, employment of a fire-extinguishing system in structures which have a central alarm system involve interfacing between the fire-extinguishing system and the building fire alarm, to allow notification of the central alarm that the fire-extinguishing system has activated. Some fire systems report directly to nearby fire stations. Communicate with building management prior to operating. Fire-extinguishing systems may be interfaced with the alarm system.

Example of an alarm bell

---

[10] See NFPA 17A, Section 4.4.3

NFPA 96, Section 10.6.1: Upon activation of an automatic fire-extinguishing system, an audible alarm or visual indicator shall be provided to show that the system has activated.

10.6.2 Where a fire alarm signaling system is serving the occupancy where the extinguishing system is located, the activation of the automatic fire-extinguishing system shall activate the fire alarm signaling system.

All electrical extinguishing systems must have auxiliary alarms or backup power for the detection line.

UL 300 requires alarm tie-in and/or 90db bell activation upon discharge.

System Supervision

NFPA 96, Section 10.7 requires:

- Where electrical power is required, it shall be monitored by a supervisory alarm, with a standby power supply provided

- Supervision is not required where the fire-extinguishing system has automatic mechanical detection and actuation as backup

- Supervision is not required where the fire-extinguishing system is interconnected or interlocked with the cooking appliance power sources so if the extinguishing system becomes inoperable due to power failure, the fuel sources and electric power are automatically shut off

Distribution System

The most important part of the distribution system is the nozzles.

Nozzles

The primary function of the nozzle is to ensure proper delivery of chemical agent to the appliances, hoods, plenum and duct area.

Two examples of "rings" that indicate the flow rate of the nozzle

Each nozzle is designed to distribute the agent in a specific pattern. Nozzles have permanent markings, which can be used to identify the manufacturer, type of nozzle, and its spray pattern. Discharge nozzles must be specifically listed for their use. This information will assist in verifying the correct application of the nozzle for the cooking equipment protected. Further it is critical that the nozzle be aimed in the proper direction.

Nozzle Ratings: Nozzles have different flow rates (the amount or volume of wet chemical that will "flow" through the nozzle). Check with the fire-extinguishing installer for the ratings of each nozzle.

All manufacturers provide nozzle covers or blow-off caps. These protect the small discharge orifice from becoming plugged with grease and dirt.

Two examples of nozzle covers. The picture on the left has a circle to indicate the blow-off cover.

NFPA 17A requires that all nozzles have greasetight caps (steel or high temperature rubber).

One manufacturer requires a thin layer of Dow Corning 101 silicone to be applied to the nozzle orifice.

The major problem with nozzles is that the covers (caps) fall off easily. If they are off for an extended period of time, grease can buildup and plug the small orifice of the distribution nozzle. When it discharges, the amount or the direction of the agent can be altered.[11]

Both fixed pipe fire-extinguishing nozzles and water sprinkler systems should have their protective caps checked and replaced if they are found to be missing.

---

[11] For further specific information on Fire-Extinguishing Equipment, NFPA 96, Chapter 10, NFPA 13, NFPA 17 and NFPA 17A, and IMC Section 509.

Automatic Water Sprinklers

Automatic sprinkler systems are also used for the protection of commercial cooking equipment and exhaust systems. NFPA 96 references the sprinkler standard, NFPA 13 *Standard for the Installation of Sprinkler Systems*, which specifies design criteria and installation rules in Section 7.9. Sprinklers are not required in ducts, duct collars, and plenum chambers if listed grease hoods serve all cooking equipment.

There are also other exceptions noted for sprinkler protection of ducts. As is the case with pre-engineered wet chemical extinguishing systems, the activation of the sprinkler must shut down the sources of fuel to the cooking equipment.

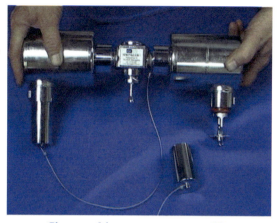

Close up of the new automatic sprinkler for use over deep fryers

There is a newer type of dual agent system designed to augment a water-based sprinkler system for the protection of deep fat fryers. This system is tested and listed under the newer standard, UL 199E, *Fire Testing of Water Spray Nozzles for the Protection of Deep Fat Fryers*. This system utilizes a chemical agent with the addition of water spray, and it is listed in the UL category, *Attachments to Sprinkler Systems*. Manufacturers and engineers should be consulted for specific details on these new technology systems.

New to 2011 NFPA 96:[12]

> *11.2.7 Fixed temperature-sensing elements other than the fusible metal alloy type shall be permitted to remain continuously in service, provided they are inspected and cleaned or replaced if necessary in accordance with the manufacturer's instruction, every 12 months or more frequently to ensure proper operation of the system.*

Cooking line with automatic sprinkler

Solid Fuel Extinguishing

Solid fuel cooking appliances that produce grease-laden vapors are required to be protected by listed fire-extinguishing equipment. Fire-extinguishing equipment shall be rated and designed to extinguish solid fuel cooking fires, in accordance with the manufacturer's recommendations.

Where acceptable to the authority having jurisdiction, solid fuel-burning cooking appliances constructed of solid masonry or reinforced portland or refractory cement concrete and vented in accordance with *NFPA 211, Chapters 3 and 4, Standard for Chimneys, Fireplaces, Vents, and Solid Fuel-Burning Appliances*, shall not require fixed automatic fire-extinguishing equipment.

Hose Protection of Fire Box

Solid fuel appliances with fireboxes exceeding 0.14 m³ (5 ft³) are required to be provided with a fixed water pipe system with a hose in the kitchen capable of reaching the firebox.[13]

Results of a solid fuel fire

---

[12] For further details see Key Changes in Chapter 2, Codes.

[13] For further details, see NFPA 96, Section 14.7.

Portable Fire Extinguishers

NFPA 96, Chapter 10.10 considers the provision of portable fire extinguishers as secondary backup fire protection. It requires that the portables be installed in accordance with NFPA 10 *Standard for Portable Fire Extinguishers*, and that they be specifically listed for such use. It further requires the use of agents that saponify upon contact with hot grease.

NFPA 96 does not allow the use of Class B (fires in flammable or combustible liquids) gas-type portables in kitchen cooking areas.

> *NFPA 96, Section 10.2.2*: A placard shall be conspicuously placed near each extinguisher that states that the fire protection system shall be activated prior to using the fire extinguisher.*
>
> *10.2.2.1 The language and wording for the placard shall be approved by the authority having jurisdiction.*

Staff Training

Training is necessary in both the use of the portables but more importantly in the activation of the fixed fire suppression system. Beyond getting extinguishing agent on the appliance fire, activating the fixed system will shut the gas off to the appliances.[14]

> *NEW to the 2011 Standard NFPA 96, Section 10.5.7:*
>
> *Instructions shall be provided to employees regarding the proper use of portable fire extinguishers and of the manual activation of fire-extinguishing equipment.*

Portable Extinguishers for Solid Fuel

All solid fuel appliances (whether or not under a hood) with fireboxes of 0.14 m³ (5 ft³) volume or less shall have at least a 2-A-rated water-type or 6L (1.6 gal) wet chemical fire extinguisher listed for class K fires in accordance with *NFPA 10 Standard for Portable Fire Extinguishers*, in the immediate vicinity of the appliance.

A Fire Inspector checking the tag on a portable fire extinguisher

K-Class

NFPA 10 *Standard for Portable Fire-Extinguishers* requires that extinguishers provided for the protection of cooking appliances that use combustible cooking media, must be listed and labeled for Class K fires. Class K fires are defined as those fires in cooking appliances involving vegetable or animal oils or fats.

K-Class portables are formulated for grease fires in commercial kitchens. These wet chemical extinguishers contain a special potassium-based low pH agent (the same chemicals as in fixed pipe wet extinguishing systems). The fine spray mist prevents the splashing of the grease and can be confined to the fire surface.

Fires are extinguished by the act of saponification, which is the chemical reaction with burning grease, an act that causes the resulting mixture to foam up. This foam spreads across the grease and forms a blanket, which prevents the fire from re-flashing.

---

[14] For further details see Key Changes in Chapter 2, Codes.

NFPA 10 further requires that class K extinguishers manufactured after January 1, 2002 not be provided with extended-wand-type discharge devices. These devices, that can permit the subsurface injection of wet chemical agents into hot cooking media, are not safe for use.

Extinguishers installed for the protection of cooking appliances prior to June 30, 1988 are not required to be listed for Class K fires. Further portable requirements are:

- A placard next to the extinguisher that states the fire protection system shall be activated before using the portable extinguisher

- That dry chemical extinguishers be replaced with K Class listed types when the dry chemical extinguishers are due for 6-year maintenance or hydrostatic test

- The maximum travel distance shall not exceed 30 ft. from the hazard to the extinguisher

- Class B gas-type portables shall not be permitted in kitchen cooking areas

- Manufacturer's recommendations shall be followed

- Other fire extinguishers in the kitchen area shall be installed in accordance with NFPA 10, *Standard for Portable Fire Extinguishers*

Non-Compliant Extinguishing Systems

Grease Buildup

One of the primary causes of fire-extinguishing system malfunction is grease buildup. Even if the fire-extinguishing system is installed correctly, it will not function properly if there is sufficient grease buildup. These systems must function under severe circumstances. The following pictures are examples of the grease load that these systems can accumulate if not properly maintained. The kitchen staff must keep an eye on the grease buildup on the fire-extinguishing system; if it is impacted the service company needs to be called.

A grease coated link assembly (links are required to be changed semi-annually as per NFPA 96)

Examples of fusible link assemblies and nozzles completely encrusted in grease

A fusible link assembly and nozzle directed up the duct completely encrusted in grease

A completely impacted extinguishing system in the plenum of an oriental kitchen. Courtesy of Bryan's Exhaust Cleaning.

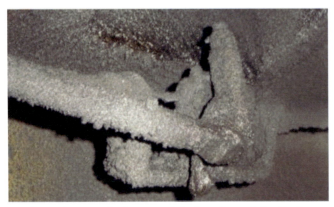

Grease has completely encased the detection and distribution components. Additionally, this system is improperly installed. The nozzle location will interfere with the ability of the fusible link to detect heat rise.

A comparison of block of grease on left to what is under the grease on right. This was the duct protection above a charbroiler. This picture was taken just after the fire-extinguishing system was allegedly serviced.

Non-Compliant Dry Chemical Systems

NFPA 96 continues to <u>allow</u> existing dry chemical extinguishing systems to exist if the original cooking line and other factors have not changed.

Dry chemical systems have <u>not</u> been listed for kitchen exhaust use since 1994. Manufacturers do <u>not</u> support the use of these systems.

An old fashion type of dry chemical nozzles – with cap and without (used for charbroiler protection)

Dry chemical system with a broken pipe that would not work

Dry chemical system with the piping blocking the closure of the non-compliant mesh filter

Other Non-Compliant Issues

Improperly wired extinguishing system control components. Installation and service should only be performed by properly trained individuals.

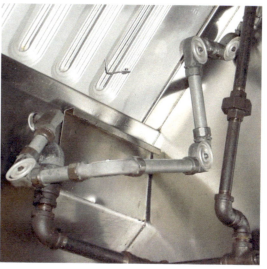

A ridiculous installation. Every elbow increases the possibility of a jamming of the cable.

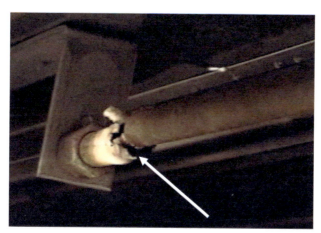

Equipment in a restaurant near the sea; the salt air corroded the cable pull

The release cable (EMT) elbow disconnected from the piping. The cable could become jammed in this situation

Example of a fire that was not contained by faulty dry chemical system

THIS PAGE HAS BEEN INTENTIONALLY LEFT BLANK

Chapter Six - Ducts and Fans

Ductwork

The ductwork is similar to the drainpipe of our bathtub example used earlier. It carries heat and vapor out of the building.

NFPA 96, Chapter 7 is one of the most extensive in the Standard. IMC 506.3 also covers duct installation and for the most part, reflects NFPA 96 Standards. It includes information on metal thickness, access, interior and exterior installations, enclosures, and termination requirements.

General duct requirements according to NFPA 96, Section 7.1 through 7.6:

- Ducts must be constructed of 16-gauge carbon steel 0.054 in. (1.37 mm) or 18-gauge stainless steel 0.043 in. (1.09 mm). Experts have determined that this thickness of metal will withstand and contain the heat of an internal fire.

- All duct seams shall be liquidtight (greasetight) and continuous welded. Greasetight is defined as not allowing the passage of grease through the seams under normal cooking conditions.

- It is imperative that grease exhaust ducts be treated as if they will be chimneys for fire, not just air conditioning ductwork. Therefore they must not pass through building firewalls.

- Exhaust ductwork cannot physically join other ducting systems (such as HVAC)

- In most cases, ducts need to have enclosures (protective clearance from combustible shafts) within the building

- When two exhaust ducts are joined together, the bottom edges shall be flush; therefore, no dips or valleys should exist where grease can accumulate and cause a firetrap

Installation

Ducts are installed in two ways. On single story buildings, the duct may arrive from a sheet metal shop in one long piece. In other cases and on multi-story buildings, sections of pre-made (approx 121.9 cm or 4 ft) ductwork are welded together onsite. In either case it is <u>imperative</u> to confirm that all welds are liquidtight.

A solidly welded duct is defined as a continuous, uninterrupted duct that has been installed in sections and then welded together on site. Smooth internal welding is permitted.

In reality most welded ductwork leaks. Testing prior to occupancy with light or pressure-testing will confirm that leaks exist. It may take multiple tests to locate all leaks. Should the duct be covered or concealed (enclosed) in some way, grease that leaks out will build up behind the insulation and create a hidden fire hazard.

NFPA 96, Section 7.5.5.1: Acceptable duct-to-duct connection shall be as follows:

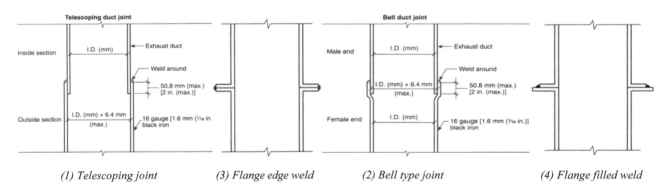

(1) Telescoping joint　　　*(3) Flange edge weld*　　　*(2) Bell type joint*　　　*(4) Flange filled weld*

Telescoping and Bell Type Connections

- The inside duct section shall always be uphill of the outside duct section

- The difference between inside dimensions of overlapping sections shall not exceed 6.4 mm (0.25 in.)

- The overlap shall not exceed 50.8 mm (2 in.)

Butt-welded connections are <u>not</u> permitted. This style of connections generally results in a poor union of the two ducts sections. This in turn creates leakage. If this type of weld is encountered it is imperative that the duct be pressure or liquid tested.

Exterior Installations

More information on this subject can be found at NFPA 96, Section 7.6.

- Ductwork on the exterior of a building shall be vertical wherever possible and adequately supported

- Duct material subject to corrosion should have limited contact with the building

- Fasteners that support the vertical duct to the building (bolts, screws, rivets, and other mechanical fasteners) shall not penetrate duct walls

- Non-stainless steel ducts shall be protected on the exterior by paint or other suitable weather-protective coating

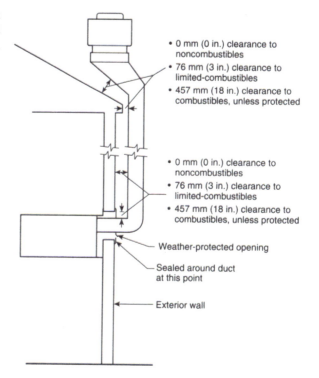

- 0 mm (0 in.) clearance to noncombustibles
- 76 mm (3 in.) clearance to limited-combustibles
- 457 mm (18 in.) clearance to combustibles, unless protected

- 0 mm (0 in.) clearance to noncombustibles
- 76 mm (3 in.) clearance to limited-combustibles
- 457 mm (18 in.) clearance to combustibles, unless protected

- Weather-protected opening
- Sealed around duct at this point
- Exterior wall

Long Horizontal Ducting

Ducts must be constructed and installed so that grease cannot collect in low spots. In long horizontal ducts, a slope is required of 6.4 mm (0.25 in.) over 305 mm (12 in.). Additionally, it must drain into an approved grease reservoir. In some areas a pitch of 1 inch may be required with accompanying approved sumps. Check local by-laws for these requirements.

Kitchen exhaust ductwork shall be rigidly fastened to the framing of the building. Support systems for horizontal grease ducts 609 mm (24 in.) and larger shall be designed for the weight of entrants up to 363 kg (800 lb) at any point in the duct systems.

However, it is not uncommon that over time, buildings will settle. If this happens, the rigid fastening can cause the duct to crack, resulting in leakage of grease. This can be a contributing factor in spread of fire within the building. This is particularly important if there are large horizontal sections.

Several long horizontal round ducts

Multiple Duct Exhaust Systems

Single story buildings such as freestanding restaurants will commonly exhaust through single systems (one hood, one duct, one fan). This arrangement allows for good balancing for proper operation and energy savings.

In multiple story buildings, it is common to connect multiple hoods into one exhaust duct that terminates on the roof of the building. The size of the duct inside the building increases in size as each hood enters the common duct. ASHRAE recommends that all turns in the duct should curve rather than have abrupt 90-degree changes in direction. Abrupt turns will result in turbulence and additional grease deposition.

Using one duct and fan to operate several hoods can create air-balancing problems at the individual hood locations.

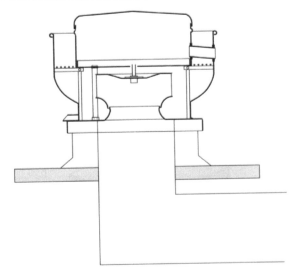

Example of a change of direction too close to the fan

It is widely recognized that multiple ducts systems need to be designed, tested and balanced by qualified professionals.

> *NFPA 96, Section 8.4.1*: Master kitchen exhaust ducts that serve multiple tenants shall include provision to bleed air from outdoors or from adjacent spaces into the master exhaust duct where required to maintain the necessary minimum air velocity in the master exhaust duct.*

Further requirements of multiple duct applications are found at NFPA 96, Section 8.4:

- The bleeder air duct must be installed on the top or the side of the main (master) exhaust duct. Installation is not allowed on the bottom of the main duct.

- The bleed air duct requires a fire damper at least 304.8 mm (12 in.) from the exhaust duct connection

- The bleed air duct must have the same construction and clearance requirements as the main exhaust duct at least 304.8 mm (12 in.) on both sides of the fire damper

- Bleed ducts must have adjustable air volume dampers

- Bleed duct shall not be used for kitchen exhaust purposes

- Unused tenant exhaust connections to the master exhaust duct that are not used as bleed air connections shall be disconnected and sealed at the main duct

- If there are multiple hoods there must be inspection access openings in the duct. It is important to identify the locations these access openings.

Clearances to Combustibles

NFPA 96, Section 4.2 and IMC 506.3.6 discuss clearances where enclosures are not required. The three accepted clearance to combustible distances are 457 mm (18 in.) to combustibles, 76 mm (3 in.) to limited combustibles, and 0 mm (0 in.) to noncombustibles.

Where the hood, duct or grease removal devices are listed, the listing requirements shall be permitted.

For more on *Clearance Reductions and Listed Materials* – see Protection from Heat (Enclosures) in this chapter.

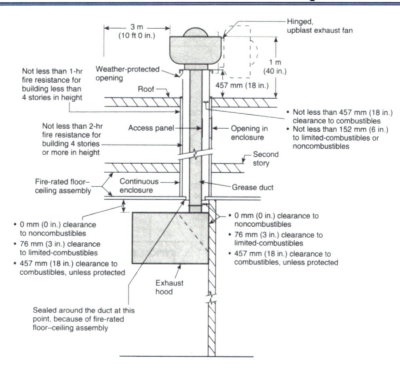

NFPA 96 Drawing of various clearance requirements

Non-Compliant Ductwork

Over the past 50 years a number of types and a variety of metal thickness of ductwork have been used. Some forms are no longer accepted in Building Codes in most regions.

However, because of grandfathering a considerable percentage of inferior ducting continues in use today. NFPA 96, IMC and other Standards such as Sheet Metal Air-Conditioning Contractors National Association (SMACNA), provide construction requirements for ductwork.

Bolted and Screwed Ducts

Bolted ducts may be made of heavy steel, and therefore slightly more self-contained than S-lock ducting. However, they are non-compliant because these connections will leak, creating a potential fire situation.

Whether bolted or light weight S-lock, neither can be cleaned properly because of leakage.

An example of bolted ductwork

Thin "hardware store" stove pipe being used over a grease-producing stove.
Note the screw in center of the picture on the right.

Another example of ductwork being screwed together, this time using air conditioning ductwork in addition to standard steel ductwork

Typical screw connected leaking duct

"S-Lock" Joint

Some older buildings still have lightweight, galvanized ducts, basically nothing more than air conditioning ductwork. These ducts are joined together with only strips of metal, called S-joints (sometimes called "Pittsburgh Seams"). These are not liquidtight and therefore non-compliant.

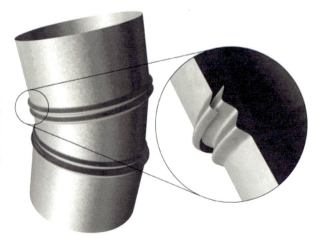

Example of an S-lock duct

Aluminum Ducts

In some areas, non-compliant aluminum flex tubing has actually been allowed. These vents are commonly used for clothes dryer venting. Obviously they will not stand up in a fire.

An aluminum hood and duct that is connected by folding the metal of the two components together

An example of aluminum dryer vent used in a kitchen exhaust application

A grease impacted, non welded duct with the electrical conduit running through it

This access panel leaked so bad – a plastic garbage bag was attached to catch grease

A hood to duct connection done with duct tape. Note: not that it matters but the duct tape is UL listed.

An aluminum duct that is only crimped together

Gaps and Holes

Any opening in the duct will reduce the efficiency of the draw of the fan, (static pressure) and will provide oxygen for a fire. Whether rusted out or intentionally cut access openings have to be properly sealed.

The rust corrosion on this outside duct rotted completely through

Looking down at a rust hole in the bottom of a duct. This hole was at the base of a vertical riser on the outside of a building.

Penetrations

This exhaust duct in the attic of a hospital has a gas pipe running through the middle of it

The exhaust cleaner cut a hole in the duct to get his pressure washer wand in the duct and fan

This hole was left open when the fire-extinguishing piping was changed out

Non-Compliant Clearances

The distance of the duct to combustibles is without a doubt the greatest hidden danger in exhaust systems. A fire can quickly ignite hidden combustibles that are hard to reach. As an inspector, if you can make the effort to get up into sub ceilings or roof, you will be able to see this problem.

An exhaust duct running right next to a wooden roof truss

A duct and the back of a hood with numerous clearance issues. The hood is held up by 2x4's, the duct is b-vent, and the duct elbow is held together with duct tape.

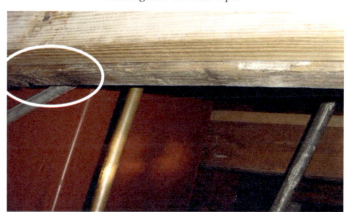

A wooden roof truss next to a kitchen exhaust duct. Note the wood is darkening from radiant heat from the duct. The ignition temperature of this wood will be much lower than normal wood. Courtesy of Bernard Besal.

Wood in Ductwork

Beyond the error of combustibles too close to ducts and fans, in some cases sheer negligence involves using wood to complete the exhaust system. This often happens when the fan has to sit up above the roof. Contractors will simply set lumber on edge to create height above the roof surface. This wood will obviously become saturated with grease and constitute an excellent fuel source if a fire in the duct reaches it.

An aluminum duct folded back and screwed to the horizontal wooden ceiling from outside

This duct had 2x6's used to created a box for the fan. This is very typical.

A duct that was made, in part, out of wood

The grease duct was only extended 6 inches above the roof with no clearance to the wood rafters

Protection from Heat (Enclosures)

All Standards and Codes recognize the danger of radiant heat, from the hood and duct, reaching combustible materials (building or stored).[1]

NFPA 96, Section 7.7.1.1: In all buildings where vertical fire barriers are penetrated, the ducts shall be enclosed in a continuous enclosure extending from the first penetrated fire barrier and any subsequent fire barriers or concealed spaces, to or through the exterior, so as to maintain the fire resistance rating of the highest fire barrier penetrated.

7.7.1.2 In all buildings more than one story in height, and in one-story buildings where the roof-ceiling assembly is required to have a fire resistance rating, the ducts shall be enclosed in a continuous enclosure extending from the lowest fire-rated ceiling or floor above the hood, through any concealed spaces, to or through the roof so as to maintain the integrity of the fire separations required by the applicable building code provisions.

7.7.1.3 The enclosure shall be sealed around the duct at the point of penetration of the first fire-rated barrier after the hood in order to maintain the fire resistance rating of the enclosure.

For most duct installations, NFPA 96 and IMC require a continuous enclosure (shaft) of the duct from the ceiling in the kitchen to the roof or fan. The purpose of an enclosure is to protect the building structure and any combustibles from coming into close contact with the duct. This serves two purposes. Over time heat that radiates from the duct can dry wooden structures (called pyrolysis). This lowers the ignition temperature of the wood. If there is a flare-up in the duct, causing a rapid increase in radiant heat, the dried wood can more easily be ignited. Additionally, by having a duct enclosure with an air space around the duct, the radiant heat of a fire will be less severe and stored boxes or building structures near the enclosure will be able to better withstand the fire.

Very poorly installed duct wrap. Installers should provide some documentation that they are factory trained or authorized

---

[1] See IMC 506.3.11, Duct Enclosures.

Examples of traditional fire-rated duct enclosure materials:

- Gypsum board (drywall, gyproc)
- Plaster
- Concrete
- Ceramic tiles

Other duct enclosure codes and standards to be aware of:

- The protection methods for ducts to reduce clearance shall be applied to the combustible or limited-combustible construction, not to the duct itself

2-hour Gypsum board fire wall

- The vast majority of exhaust duct enclosures are made of limited combustible material (usually gypsum board on steel studs). These enclosures are built on site.

Listed Duct Enclosures

Commonly there are two types of listed duct enclosures: Field-Applied enclosures are commonly called "duct wrap" and Factory-Built grease ducts which are double walled steel ducts with insulation between the walls.

These manufactured systems are required to be in conformance with the recent UL 2221, *Standard for Tests of Fire Resistive Grease Duct Enclosure Assemblies* or equivalent.

Grease Duct Enclosure definitions:

> *NFPA 96, Section 3.3.23.2.1 Factory-Built Grease Duct Enclosures. A listed factory-built grease duct system evaluated as an enclosure system for reduced clearances to combustibles and as an alternative to a duct with its fire-rated enclosure.*

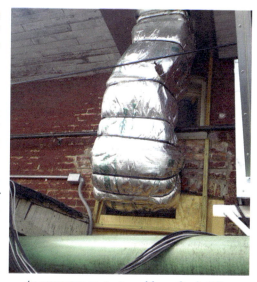

An attempt to protect an old wooden building from the grease exhaust duct.

> *3.3.23.2.2 Field-Applied Grease Duct Enclosure. A listed system evaluated for reduced clearances to combustibles and as an alternative to a duct with its fire-rated enclosure.*

NFPA 96, Section 4.3 and 7.7 discuss the application of listed Field-Applied and Factory-Built Grease Duct Enclosures. These manufactured systems are generally used to reduce the clearances to zero. These listed assemblies do <u>not</u> need to correspond with the clearance requirements of NFPA 96, Section 4.2.

> *NFPA 96, Section 7.7.2.2.3 Provisions for reducing clearances as described in Section 4.2 shall not be applicable to enclosures.*

On listed enclosures the material may touch the exterior of the duct. Additionally, the outermost surface of the enclosure material is considered non-combustible.

Clearance options for field-applied and factory-built grease duct enclosures shall be in accordance with the listing of the material used. The manufacturer should be consulted and whatever the clearance options are should be identified in the listing and installation instructions.

Inspectors should require manufacturers and the installing contractor to confirm, in writing, that all the conditions and procedures of the <u>installation</u> are covered under the listing, before allowing the system to be installed. When the installation is complete, require documentation.

Protection of Coverings and Enclosure Materials

NFPA 96, Section 7.7.3 states that measures shall be taken to prevent physical damage to any covering or enclosure material. Any damage to the covering or enclosure shall be repaired and restored to meet its listing and fire resistive rating.

Field-Applied Grease Duct Enclosures

Field-applied grease duct enclosures are commonly called duct wrap, or fire barriers. These are generic terms for listed material, products and systems that envelope a grease duct for the purpose of reducing clearances to combustible construction and as an alternative to traditional fire rated shaft enclosures.

Field-applied enclosures generally come in two forms: Flexible and Rigid. Flexible wraps are made of ceramic fiber blankets, which basically cocoon the duct. Rigid board is made of calcium silicate, and can be used to construct a solid "rigid" frame around the duct, similar to a traditional duct shaft enclosure.

Duct enclosures make it difficult to inspect the duct. Their listing and application require that they completely cover or "enclose" the duct, making it difficult to visually inspect whether the duct is leaking, or if there are access panels that have been covered over by the wrap.

Duct wrap products may be useful when an inspector finds pre-existing kitchen exhaust ductwork that is too close to combustible structures. This would protect areas in heritage buildings or other locations where adequate clearance is simply not available.

Listed Field-applied grease duct enclosures can be installed around ducts to provide reduced clearances. Where you encounter listed manufactured field-applied duct enclosures, contact the manufacturer for further details.

Two examples of different brands of field-applied grease duct enclosures (duct wrap)

Factory-Built Grease Ducts

All types of factory-built systems must be listed for the application, tested at 1093ºC (2000ºF) and have designations for reduced clearance to combustibles. Listed prefabricated grease ducts are factory built, assembled in the field and require no welding.

These round ducts are constructed to be liquidtight. Provisions are made for grease duct clean-out openings.

Listed factory-built grease duct systems are joined by means of a mechanical clamp.

Joint designs are tested by Underwriters Laboratories for liquid tightness.[2]

A factory-built duct enclosure

---

[2] Refer to UL 1978 "Grease Ducts", Section 16, Leakage Test

Factory-built grease ducts are designed to include adjustable length duct sections that expand and contract during changes in exhaust temperatures.

This orientation shall allow cleaning solutions to flow downhill without being trapped between gaps. Manufacturer's installation instructions will specify the direction that such pipe sections are to be orientated.

Examples of factory-built grease duct enclosures. Removing the tightening band and examining the interior security connection. Courtesy of Metal-Fab, Inc.

Non-Compliant Duct Wrap

Improperly installed duct wrapping or wrapping ducts that have leaks can create a serious issue. The system owner will be under the assumption that the wrap protects the ducts, when in fact it is not. In the case of leaking ducts, the grease that leaks out will not be visible to inspection. In serious cases, if there is a fire the wrap will be compromised.

Duct wrap concealing a leaking vertical duct

An exhaust cleaning company came in and tore all the wrap off looking for an access panel. They didn't find one and left.

 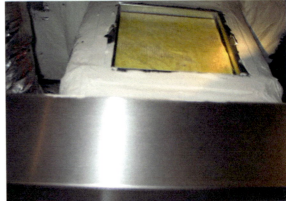

An unsafe HVAC access panel on a wrapped duct. This type of panel would not withstand the intensity of a serious duct fire. But not to worry, the installer never actually created an opening!

The duct wrap was not replaced at an access panel by the fan

The duct wrap has been intentionally pulled away from the bottom of the duct to find the leak

Although the access panel was not wrapped, this one withstood the fire in reasonably good condition. The roof was steel.

Access

Inadequate access into the duct continues to be one of the most severe fire hazards in kitchen exhaust systems. Without proper access, the complete removal of combustible grease buildup is not possible. This is one of the most important NFPA 96 and IMC requirements.

Note: Because of the importance of access, some NFPA 96 quotes are intentionally repeated in this section.

> *NFPA 96, Section 4.1.8: All interior surfaces of the exhaust system shall be reasonably accessible for cleaning and inspection purposes.*

> *IMC 506.3.9 Cleanouts and other openings: Any portion of such system having sections not provided with access from the duct entry or discharge shall be provided with cleanout openings.*

Many exhaust systems are not designed or installed to allow for sufficient access. Often where access is installed, it is subsequently obstructed by other construction (such as plumbing, electrical, framing, etc.).

Access openings (entryways) need to be installed so that the entire system can be safely inspected and thoroughly cleaned. Access panels need to be installed at a frequency that a worker can clean all portions of the system. Openings on horizontal and vertical ducts must have safe access and a work platform when not easily accessible from the floor or a 3 m (10 ft) stepladder.

NEW to NFPA 96, 2011 Edition:[3]

> *Section 7.4.2.3 If not easily accessible from the floor or a 3 m (10 ft) stepladder, openings on vertical grease ducts shall be provided with safe access and a work platform.*

NFPA and IMC compliant access panels. Courtesy of Flame Gard CHG.

Duct Openings for Cleaning and Inspections

Openings

Openings shall be installed to NFPA 96, Sections 7.3 and 7.4 and IMC 506.3.9.

- Openings shall be on the sides or top of the duct, whichever is more accessible[4]

- Access is required at changes of direction (elbows)

- Openings are not required where the duct is accessible from the duct entry or discharge

- The edge of openings shall be at least 38.1 mm (1.5 in.) from all outside edges of the duct or welded seams. Practicality calls for never going closer than 38.1 mm (1.5 in.) to any edge, since this compromises the duct and does not give a secure bite for panel installation.

- Where the horizontal duct is large enough, an access panel a minimum of 50.8 x 50.8 cm (20 x 20 in.) that allows personnel entry should be installed on each floor. Where the duct is too small, openings are required every 3.7 m (12 ft).[5]

- Hoods with dampers in the exhaust or supply collar shall have an access panel (opening) for cleaning and inspection in the duct or the hood collar within 457 mm (18 in.) of the damper

- This Standard is meant to provide access in certain dampered hood systems that block off the ability to do cleaning of the duct, because of the location of the damper in the throat of the duct. In practical terms, this access is rarely installed, meaning inspections and cleaning is difficult or impossible above the hood dampers.

---

[3] For further details see Key Changes in Chapter 2, Codes.

[4] IMC allows for access on the bottom of ducts but only in very specific situations with proper construction restraints. See IMC 506.3.10.

[5] IMC 506.3.10 allows access openings to be installed only every 6.1 meters (20 ft), which is a major difference from the NFPA.

- If there is additional ductwork extending past the fan (upstream), access is required in the duct within 3 feet of the fan on either side for inspection and cleaning. This gives adequate access to both sides of the fan.

Vertical ducts capable of personal entry require access only on the top of the vertical riser. Where entry is not possible, access must be on every floor.

Note: If access is not available on every floor the duct may still be able to be properly cleaned with the use of a high-powered pressure washer and a "Spin-Jet."

In many cases, other equipment, plumbing, wiring and what not is installed in such a way as to block access. Inspectors need to be on the look out for blocked access or opening.[6]

A properly installed access panel on the vertical side of a duct. Courtesy of Component Hardware Group

Access Panels

Access panels must comply with NFPA 96, Section 7.4.

- Access panels need to be either 16-gauge steel or 18-gauge stainless steel. NFPA 96, Section 7.4.3 does <u>not</u> mean access panel can be made out of inferior steel sheeting because the duct is made out of that inferior material.

- The minimum standard for Type I ducts is <u>steel</u>. This thickness of steel metal will sustain a fire.

  NFPA 96 7.4.3.2 Access panels shall have a gasket or sealant that is rated for 815.6ºC (1500ºF) and shall be greasetight.

- No flexible 'caulking-tube' type silicone is rated at 815.6°C (1500°F). This creates a dilemma with older "screw on" access panels. These panels need proper gasketing, but are not built to allow for the thickness of accepted woven gasket fabric. Gasket material must be made of aluminum silicate (most popular), or a comparable substance.

Aluminum Silicate material for gasketing

- Access panel fasteners shall be carbon steel or stainless steel and shall not penetrate the duct walls

- Screws cannot penetrate the duct. The rationale is that they create holes where grease can leak out and flames can escape in a fire. Screws are also rarely replaced properly.

- A sign shall be placed on all access panels stating the following: ACCESS PANEL - DO NOT OBSTRUCT

- IMC states that fasteners must be removable without the use of a tool

- NEW to the 2011 Standard 9.3.1.3 Equipment shall have a space provided to all access panels or doors for the safe removal and servicing of control devices, such as filters, electrostatic precipitator cells, and odor control media beds, and for cleaning of the equipment housing.

For further details see Auxiliary Equipment in Chapter 2, Codes.

---

[6] New to 2011 NFPA 96: 9.3.1.3 Equipment shall have space provided to all access panels or doors for the safe removal and servicing of control devices, such as filters, electrostatic precipitator cells, and odor control media beds, and for cleaning of the equipment housing.

Listed Access Panels

With the introduction of NFPA 96, Section 7.4.3, which states that gaskets and sealants must be rated at least 812.6°C (1500°F) degrees and that fasteners shall not penetrate the duct walls, the installation of access panels has become increasingly difficult.

> *NFPA 96, Section 7.4.3.4: Listed grease duct access door assemblies (access panels) shall be installed in accordance with the terms of the listing and the manufacturer's instructions.*

Listed access doors are designed to provide easy access to the interior of grease ducts serving commercial and institutional kitchens for cleaning and servicing.

- They remain structurally intact and leak-proof under fire conditions

- Listed access doors are designed to be factory or field installed

Component Hardware Group -- Flame Gard UL Listed Access Panel

- These access doors may be installed by welding onto new ducts, or they may be retrofitted onto existing grease ducts, without the fire hazard created by the welding process

Fire Doors – Access into Sub-Ceilings

NFPA 96, Section 7.7.4 requires properly listed fire doors be installed in enclosures, walls and sub-ceilings to reach access panels in the exhaust ductwork.

- The doors shall be readily accessible and clearly identified and labeled

- Doors shall be installed according to NFPA 80 *Standard for Fire Doors and Fire Windows*, the listing and the manufacturer's instructions and shall be acceptable to the authority having jurisdiction

- These openings must be large enough to allow either personal entry or the removal of the exhaust access panel

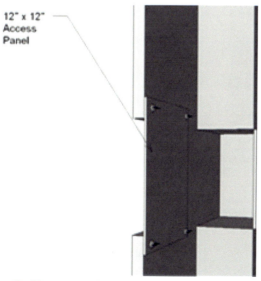

12" x 12" Access Panel

Problems arise when the fire rated enclosure door is smaller than the access panel behind it, as illustrated in the diagram above

A fire door leading to an access panel

Non-Compliant Access Panels

Non-compliant access panels may be those that are made from metal that is thinner or of lower quality then the compliant duct, such as:

- Thin galvanized sheet metal
- Aluminum flashing

Access panels that have simple tech screws (sheet metal screws) that attach the access panel to the duct are non-compliant. The use of silicone caulking to seal access panels is non-compliant.

An opening in the duct where the access panel was not replaced after cleaning

An access panel incorrectly installed on the bottom of the ductwork

Access panels on the outside of a duct at the top of a three-story building. This opening is not safely accessible.

A vertical duct over five stories high with no access possible

*No access in the upstream
section of the duct beyond the fan*

*A poorly placed access panel, which is
also installed incorrectly with screws*

*A flimsy access panel with two latches
and a "hinge" of duct tape*

*An "access panel" made completely of
strips of cloth duct tape*

*A before and after cleaning of a non-compliant light weight galvanized duct with
wooden beams running through it. Also note the electrical cable.*

An access panel secured by duct tape

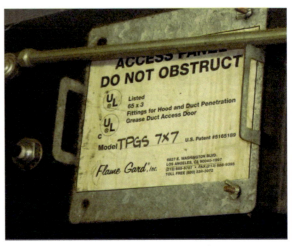

An obstructed access panel

Access Summary

Non-compliant systems are a serious fire hazard. If there is a fire, the degree of damage will be exacerbated by the various flaws in the system. If the building is made of wood or combustible material there is a good chance that it will be destroyed. Older wooden buildings pose an additional life-safety hazard to fire fighters.

- Reduced clearances can lead to pyrolysis, lowering the ignition temperatures of surrounding materials

- Inadequate access leads to incomplete cleaning, there will be areas where the combustible grease accumulate

- Fans that do not tip or are otherwise inaccessible will create buildup within and below

- Unsafe access to fans means they are likely not being cleaned

- Grease saturated roofs around the fan pose an additional fire hazard

An aluminum cookie sheet used as a makeshift access panel

Fans

Terminations

In most cases it is superior to have the exhaust system terminate on the roof of the building, as opposed to the wall. The fan should be as close to the end of the ductwork as possible to reduce air pressure on the system.

Shorter distances from the hood to the fan (as in single story buildings) require less fan power. Multi-story buildings require more fan power because of the air resistance, length and sizing of the duct.

An upblast fan

Rooftop Terminations

Rooftop terminations of either the duct or fan shall comply with NFPA 96, Section 7.8.2 and IMC 506.3.13.

- A minimum of 3.05 m (10 ft) horizontally from outlet to adjacent buildings, property lines and air intakes

- A minimum of 1.5 m (5 ft) from the outlet (the duct discharge or fan housing) to any combustible structure

- Have a vertical separation of 0.92 m (3 ft) below any exhaust outlets for air intakes within 3.05 m (10 ft) of the exhaust outlet

- The ductwork shall be a minimum of 0.46m (18 in.) away from any roof surface. On pitched roofs this measurement must be taken from the closest point between edge of fan/duct connection and the roof surface.

- Near the termination of the exhaust (whether fan or duct outlet) some form of grease collection must be provided

- The collection container must be noncombustible, closed, rainproof, and structurally sound for the service

- There must be safe access to and safe work surface to the fan and termination. There are many locations where access and working conditions around the fan are unsafe. These fans are considered inaccessible.

NFPA 96, Section A.7.8.2.2 Appendix states that all roof fans should have access to all sides from a flat roof surface without a ladder, or be provided with safe access via stairs or walkway, or a portable ladder to a flat work surface on all sides of the fan.

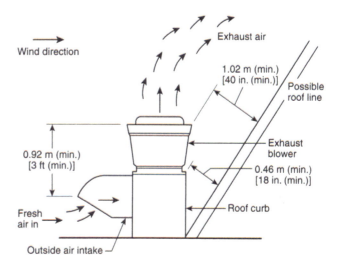

NFPA 96 drawing of various fan placement requirements

Wall Termination

Wall Terminations shall be in accordance with NFPA 96, Section 7.8.3.

- Wall terminations shall be through a noncombustible wall with a minimum of 3.05 m (10 ft) of clearance from the outlet to adjacent buildings, property lines, grade level, combustible construction, electrical equipment, and the closest point of any air intake or operable door or window

- In secured areas, a lower height above grade may be permitted

- The exhaust flow shall be directed perpendicularly outward (straight out) from the wall or upward

NFPA 96, Section A.7.8.2.2 Appendix states that all through-the-wall exhaust fans should have ready access from the ground from no more than a 1.8 m (6 ft) step ladder or should be provided with a flat work surface under the fan that allows for access to all sides of the fan, accessible from no more than a 6 m (20 ft) extension ladder.

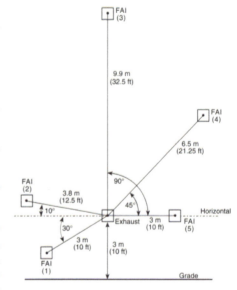

NFPA 96 drawing of distances required to fresh air intakes

Two examples of wall terminations

Grease Collection

On wall terminations, some means of collection must be in place. Either the duct needs to be pitched back into the building (to the hood) or have a collection container or trap (in or outside the building).

General Fan Requirements

There are various types of fans available for exhausting the hot and contaminated air produced by the cooking process. NFPA 96, Chapter 8 and IMC 506.5 identify factors that need to be considered regarding fans:

- Fan selection should be based on its ability to overcome frictional, distance, airflow resistance and move appropriate amounts of air desired

- The high temperatures and grease content of the air encountered in these applications make it mandatory to select a fan with the motor out of the air stream. This will prevent grease buildup or excessive temperatures, which will cause motor burnout.

Typical upblast type fan

- Fans need to be designed to direct air away from the rooftop (or, in the case of wall termination fans, away from the building) to prevent roof and building damage

- Drains and collectors must be used to catch and contain any grease that may collect and drip from the fans[7]

- Fans should be as close to the termination of the duct as possible. Termination should be at or above the roofline. Fans that exhaust on walls or in enclosures can have problems with air contamination, proximity to intake or windows and backdraft issues.

- There must be safe access and work surface for inspection and cleaning. When inspecting a restaurant, the only way to know if the fan is accessible is to go and see it.

- Fans must be situated at least 46 cm (18 in.) above the roof surface and air must exhaust at least 1 m (40 in.) above the surface[8]

Fan Types

Upblast Fan

The most common fan used over exhaust systems is an aluminum upblast fan. However, as this design is used for a number of other industrial air movement applications, fans over the kitchen exhaust must be listed for this specific purpose. Upblast fans shall be installed in accordance with NFPA 96, Sections 7.8.2.1 (4,5,8) and 8.1.1.1.

Editorial Note: From outward appearance it is impossible to tell if an upblast fan is listed for the purpose. An inspector must read the listing label found in the motor housing. Fans must be:

- UL Listed for commercial cooking use[9]

- Able to drain grease out of any trap or low point into a non-combustible container or collection device. The collection system shall not inhibit the performance of the fan.

- Hinged and have a flexible weatherproof electrical cable to allow for cleaning[10]

Poorly installed hinge kit. If you look closely see the electrical cable prevents the hinge from opening.

Aluminum upblast fans with proper hinge kit

---

[7] See the Grease Containment Systems Section later in this chapter.

[8] The duct must extend 18 in. above the nearest roof surface. The fan base will rest on the top of the duct.

[9] The listing label on the fan indicates if the fan is listed for commercial kitchen exhaust. Be aware that the "upblast fan" design is also used for a number of other industrial air movement applications.

[10] Because the requirement for hinge attachment is a relatively new one, many fans do not have this hinging system, making the tipping of the fan a difficult task, and the ductwork below the fan inaccessible.

Hinging and Access in Upblast Fans

In practical terms, a fan is tippable if it can be safely lifted with enough electrical cable to access underneath the fan and down the duct.

Da Hinge after market hinge kit.
Courtesy of Facilitec USA.

Proper access for an upblast fan

High Heat Applications

The recent popularity of solid cooking fuels and wood fired pizza ovens requires superior construction in fans. There are now strong cast aluminum and steel upblast style fans capable of withstanding the temperatures created by wood-fired chimneys and surviving occasional flare-ups from duct fires.

High heat application fan. Courtesy of Exhausto.

Utility Fan

Utility fans acceptable for use in commercial cooking operations should be tested by the *AMCA Testing Publication 211* and UL or ULC listed for the purpose. They shall be installed according to NFPA 96, Section 8.1.3.[11]

- Utility fans are made of steel, making them stronger and more durable than upblast fans. Utility fans can come with more powerful motors for improved lift.

- Listed utility fans are not tippable and will require access into the rear of the fan housing

- They must have grease drainage and containment

---

[11] See ASHRAE Guide and Data books.

- There must be an arrangement for grease to drain out of any low points. The grease receptacle cannot exceed 3.8 L (1 gal.).

- Utility fans are not allowed to have canvas vibration collars

- The fan must be accessible. If in an enclosure, the enclosure must be adequately fire rated.

- If there is additional ductwork extending past the fan (upstream), access is required in the duct within 0.92 m (3 ft) of the fan on either side for inspection and cleaning

 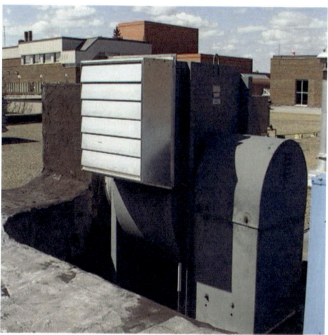

Inverse pitch or centrifugal (Utility set) fans

Inverse pitch or centrifugal (Utility set) fans

In-Line Fan

Backward inclined fan blades have higher operating efficiencies. The wheel design is strong, permitting operations at higher static pressures.

In situations such as a ground level restaurant in a 50 story high-rise building, in-line fans are the only cost effective solution. These fans are commonly found where the ductwork runs to a parking garage in large buildings or in other areas where headspace is an issue.

A cut away of an in-line (axial) fan

In-line fans shall be installed in accordance with NFPA 96, Section 8.1.2:

- In-line fans have the motor outside the air stream with the belts and pulleys protected
- Fans must be securely bolted
- Flexible canvas collars are not allowed
- There must be a means to capture grease that does not exceed 3.8 L (1 gal)
- The fan must be accessible for inspection and cleaning
- If in an enclosure, the enclosure must be fire rated
- All wiring and electrical equipment shall comply with NFPA 70

In-line (axial) fans

Non-Compliant Fans

The only way to really know that the fan is accessible and able to be maintained is to visually inspect it. The fan may be located during non-operating hours for inspection and cleaning. When the fan is reached, see if it can be tipped or accessed internally for inspection. Look for air gaps from poor contact or missing screws. Check the condition of the electrical wiring and the roof surface around the fan.

A trio of oddly modified upblast fans   *A utility fan with non-compliant access*

A two-story duct extending past a utility fan. This is not accessible for inspection or cleaning.

A wall mounted upblast fan with an aluminum box duct taped to a plastic hose that is supposed to act as a drain

Non-Compliant and Unsafe Terminations

Years ago any type of fan was allowed to exhaust kitchen air. Even today in many locations, the building department allows non-compliant fans. Poorly installed or inappropriate fans can cause serious grease buildup both in the duct (inadequate draw) or on the roof (improper discharge location and grease saturation). They may also be unsafe to access therefore making it unlikely that they will be serviced in a timely manner.

Unsafe access to the fans

An example of a fan and duct that is difficult to access and unsafe to service

NFPA 96, Section 7.8.2.2*: Fans shall be provided with safe access and work surface for inspection and cleaning.

NFPA 96, Section A.7.8.2.2: fan terminations should be accessible as follows:

- Rooftop Terminations. Fans (whether through the roof or to the roof from outside) should have safe access to all sides from a flat roof surface without a ladder, or be provided with access via built-in stairs/walkway or a portable ladder to a flat work surface on all sides of the fan.

- Wall Terminations. Through-the-wall exhaust fans should have ready access from the ground from no more than a 2-m (6-ft) stepladder or have a flat work surface under the fan that allows for access to all sides of the fan, accessible from no more than a 6.0-m (20-ft) extension ladder.

Inaccessible and unsafe fan and duct

Canvas Collars on Utility Fans

Utility fans are often found in institutions or large buildings with exhaust systems. These fans suffer from one weakness: the canvas vibration-dampening collar between the duct and the fan will disintegrate over time. When these fans are pressure washed, the water pressure can easily destroy these canvas collars.

Another reason why canvas collars are non-compliant is because in a fire they instantly burn away, allowing the fire to escape. This is a quandary because there is no easy solution.

Canvas collars are not allowed in accordance with NFPA 96.

NFPA 96, Section 8.1.3.5: Flexible connectors shall not be used.

An example of a grease-saturated canvas collar held on with duct tape

A canvas collar that burnt away in a fire, allowing the fire to escape

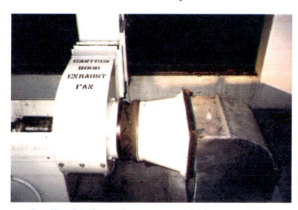

Small utility fan with a grease soaked canvas collar

A canvas collar still in good shape

Down-Blast Fans

A number of fans are not rated for use in kitchen exhaust. One, in particular, is called a down-blast fan. These are not appropriate because they blow the grease back onto the roof. A fire would be directed down onto the grease buildup.

Two examples of down-blast fans. Good demonstrations of how much grease can be expelled onto a roof from a down-blast fan.

No Hinges

Non-compliant fan without hinge systems to access the duct below the fan. Note the plywood.

Unsafe Electrical

Wiring shall be commercial grade in accordance with NFPA 70 *National Electrical Code*. Wires are <u>not</u> allowed in the ductwork.

> *NFPA 96, Section 9.2.1: Wiring systems of any type shall not be installed in ducts.*

> *9.2.2 Motors, lights, and other electrical devices shall be permitted to be installed in ducts or hoods or to be located in the path of travel of exhaust products only where specifically listed for such use.*

Non-compliant electric wiring in duct

The wiring has been stretched and damaged by lifting the fan on and off without a hinge kit

The wiring to this fan has been frayed and the protective hose has separated from repeated removing of the fan without a hinge kit

Someone's idea of an acceptable wiring job on an exhaust fan motor (this was exposed to the elements)

Grease Containment Systems

Having a grease containment system in place that traps the grease and repells water will provide considerable protection from grease damage. Additionally, having protection on the roof will keep working areas around the fan clean for service personnel.

In the past, a number of methods have been tried to protect roofing. These have taken the form of sandboxes, kitty litter, buckets and barrels of various sizes and shapes.

Many of these only collect water and overflow the grease onto the roof.

Listed fans must have integrated drain and containment boxes. Inspectors will find that most fans are not properly equipped with grease containment.

An upblast fan surrounded by rags

Grease Absorbing Roof Protection

One form of after-market grease containment system consists of a series of adsorbent polypropylene and paper filters designed to capture the different types of grease and oils. These filters should be changed regularly, according to types of cooking, accumulation, volumes and climate.[12]

Another means to capture cooking oil is a "powdered" bead-like substance that will absorb cooking oil and lock it in.

These beads will absorb approximately 4 times their weight in grease or oil and once "absorbed," will not leach the grease out. The interesting thing about these absorbent beads is that they will absorb grease, but will NOT absorb water.

The beads are also lightweight, noncombustible and safe to use and handle.

Upblast fans with grease containment systems in place. Courtesy of Impact.

Non-Compliant Roof Protection

A bad choice for grease containment: Downblast fan on sand

An example of a fan leaking grease onto the roof

---

[12] See Grease Containment Systems in the Resources Section of the Appendix, which can be downloaded from www.philackland.com/INSP2012/

THIS PAGE HAS BEEN INTENTIONALLY LEFT BLANK

Chapter Seven – Service Providers

Inspecting the work of service providers during an Inspectors Seminar in Florida.

Service Providers

Service Requirements

The maintenance of exhaust and fire-extinguishing systems is very much an out-of-sight out-of-mind service. The importance of having proper service is only emphasized after a fire.

> *NFPA 96, Section 4.1.3: The following equipment shall be kept in good working condition:*
>
> *(1) Cooking Equipment*
>
> *(2) Hoods*
>
> *(3) Ducts (if applicable)*
>
> *(4) Fans*
>
> *(5) Fire-extinguishing systems*
>
> *(6) Special Effluent or energy control equipment*
>
> *4.1.3.1 Maintenance and repairs shall be performed on all components at intervals necessary to maintain good working condition.*

If the suppression or exhaust systems are not safe they should not be operated. So many fires could have been prevented if proper maintenance had been preformed. New changes in the 2011 NFPA 96 clarify just how important maintenance is. For further details see Key Changes in Chapter 2, Codes.

> *New to NFPA 96, 2011 Edition: 11.1.6 Cooking equipment shall not be operated while its fire-extinguishing system or exhaust system is nonoperational or impaired.*
>
> *New to NFPA 96, 2011 Edition: 11.1.6.1 Where the fire-extinguishing system or exhaust system is nonoperational or impaired, the systems shall be tagged as noncompliant, and the owners or the owner's representative shall be notified in writing of the impairment.*
>
> *NFPA 96, (2008 ed.) Section 11.2.8: Where required, certificates of inspection and maintenance shall be forwarded to the authority having jurisdiction.*

Responsible service providers realize they are liable if they do not inform their customers of serious fire hazards. These hazards will vary depending on a number of circumstances.

The service requirements for appliances, fire-extinguishing and exhaust systems are handled by the following trades:

- Appliance Maintenance
- Water Wash Hood Mechanical Maintenance
- Ultraviolet Hood Maintenance
- Recirculating Systems Servicing
- Fire-Extinguishing Servicing
- Portable Extinguisher Servicing
- Damper Links
- Exhaust Cleaning

Each of these trades is separate and distinct. There are some companies that provide more than one of these services, but the work is usually done by different personnel and at different times of the day (or night).

The required qualification and competencies of these services vary. Each has some level of documentable skill requirements.

The Development of Certification

Since the 1998 edition of NFPA 96, exhaust inspections (for cleanliness) and exhaust cleaners were required to be *Trained, Qualified and Certified* (TQC) *acceptable to the authority having jurisdiction.* [1]

By 2004, these requirements were expanded to also include those who work on appliances and fire-extinguishing systems.

As of the publication of this manual, the question "*What is acceptable to the authority having jurisdiction?*" is only beginning to be defined.

Service providers in each of these fields has some understanding of what their "Standard of Care" should be. Some fields are better defined than others. This chapter will provide only a general understanding of those standards of care.

Point of interest: A one-person crew usually performs the servicing of fire-extinguishing systems, water wash hoods, and air pollution control systems. This individual would be TQC according to the listing of the component manufacturer's training and qualification standards. Regarding exhaust cleaning, crews of two or more are used. The Crew Leader (at least) should be trained, qualified and certified. Nationally, the requirement for TQC exhaust cleaner's lags the other commercial kitchen service trades. There are nationally recognized third parties training and certifying protocols available for all of these trades. [2]

Nationwide, there are large cleaning and fire-extinguishing service corporations who contract local companies to do their fire-extinguishing servicing and/or exhaust cleaning. Additionally, many local companies will use subcontractors to do the actual service/cleaning. Confirm the employment status of those who <u>actually performed</u> the work and under what company name(s) the work was done. Is the individual who actually performed the work trained, qualified and certified?

Defining Competency

Regarding servicing, the question inspectors and system owners need to ask is:

"Is a <u>Complete</u> and <u>Professional</u> Job taking place?"

Since the 2004 Edition of NFPA 96, formal definitions were developed for competent service providers. These definitions clarify whom and what is required for the AHJ to determine competency.

> **Trained:** A person who has become proficient in performing a skill reliably and safely through instruction and practice/field experience acceptable to the AHJ. Formal and/or technical training may be administered by the employer or recognized training program.

> **Qualified:** A competent and capable person or company that has met the requirements and training for a given field acceptable to the AHJ.

> **Certified:** A formally stated recognition and approval of an acceptable level of competency, acceptable to the AHJ. The manufacturer of the listed equipment being serviced or an independent third party may provide certification.

New Change to 2011 NFPA 96, 11.4 and 11.6 (Inspections and Cleaning): Requirements are that the <u>individual</u> is the one who is required to be Trained, Qualified and Certified, <u>not</u> the company.

Unfortunately this change clouds the "qualifications" which are generally considered to be adequate insurance and business license, which are held by a <u>company</u>, not necessarily an individual. [3]

Question to Inspectors: What is your department's policy toward holding any of these services responsible? For further details see page 14 in this chapter.

---

[1] See NFPA 96, Chapter 11 Procedures for the Use and Maintenance of Equipment, Annex A & B.

[2] For Phil Ackland Certification Protocol, see the Appendix, which can be downloaded from www.philackland.com/docs/INSP2012/

[3] Phil Ackland Certification (PAC) is very specific that there must be <u>at least one</u> certified individual on the cleaning or inspecting crew. If a cleaning company were to claim to be PAC and not have at least one individual on the job who is PAC, then their company qualification is void.

Trained

From a practical point of view both the servicing company and the responsible person on the actual job site (Crew Leader) requires some level of documented training.

This training should include:

- Understanding the local Fire Codes that they are working under
- Recognizing serious deficiencies in the exhaust or fire-extinguishing system
- How to communicate deficiencies or other issues back to the property owner
- Safety issues related to their trade
- Where applicable – How to repair systems

Qualified

These qualifications may not determine the skill level of a particular worker regardless of the service provided but may assist in assessing the effort a company is making to maintain a professional business status:

- Factory Authorized Training or Certification
- General Liability Insurance
- Business License
- Worker's Compensation (State/Industrial) Number

Other Qualifications:

- Material Safety Data Sheet (MSDS) (USA) Training and Certification
- Workplace Hazardous Material Information System (WHMIS) (Canada) Training and Certification
- Specific equipment training
- A written lockout, ladder, confined space, or other safety issues policy

Certified

Certification is the process of documenting proven training and qualifications.

The overall industry objective of TQC is to achieve a level of competency that is acceptable to all Authorities Having Jurisdiction and the restaurant industry.

Appliance Maintenance

Because appliance controls are subject to breakage and wear they require regular scheduled maintenance. Burners and heater coils must be kept free of combustible deposits. Gaskets that prevent grease from running into areas where ignitions sources exist must be properly maintained and re-installed after maintenance. Temperature controls must be periodically examined to ensure that no unauthorized "repairs" which could impair the operation of safety devices, have taken place.

Appliance location should be evaluated periodically, to ensure that the appliance is still protected by the fire-extinguishing system.[4]

---

[4] For more information on the responsibilities of food service equipment contact the Commercial Food Equipment Service Association (http://www.cfesa.com).

NFPA 96, Section 11.7.1: An inspection and servicing of the cooking equipment shall be made at least annually by properly trained, qualified persons.

11.7.2 Cooking equipment that collects grease below the surface, behind the equipment, or in cooking equipment flue gas exhaust, such as griddles or charbroilers, shall be inspected and, if found with grease accumulation, cleaned by a properly trained, qualified, and certified person acceptable to the authority having jurisdiction.

12.1.2.1 All listed appliances shall be installed in accordance with the terms of their listings and the manufacturer's instructions.

A large number of the fires that take place in kitchens are caused by equipment failure of some sort, particularly deep fryers.[5]

Listed Exhaust Systems Maintenance

Listed exhaust hoods and their components need to be maintained in accordance with the manufacturers instruction.

New Change to NFPA 96, 2011 Edition: 11.5 Inspection, <u>Testing,</u> and Maintenance of Listed Hoods Containing Mechanical, Water Spray or Ultraviolet Devices.

Listed hoods containing mechanical or fire-actuated dampers, internal washing components, or other mechanically operated devices shall be inspected and tested by properly trained qualified <u>and certified</u> persons every 6 months or at frequencies recommended by the manufacturer in accordance with their listings.

A large number of listed hoods are not receiving mechanical maintenance. When inspectors encounter listed hoods containing any mechanical device, or they should require the owner to provide proof of mechanical maintenance. For further details see Key Changes in Chapter 2, Codes.

Water Wash Hood Service Technicians

All major water wash hood manufacturers train selected service companies in the mechanical operations of their hoods.

Note: Nearly all these manufacturers also make listed non-water wash hoods that contain fire actuated dampers and other controls. Hoods with fire-actuated dampers also require regular maintenance by trained personnel.

Water wash hoods require a Start-Up Test. This written report should be on file with the restaurant, and installing company (possibly also the building department or the hood manufacturer).

Servicing

On water wash hoods the installing company is usually the same as the service company. Periodic maintenance services will be documented and should be available to inspectors.

---

[5] See the Deep Fat Fryer Section in Chapter 3, Appliances.

NFPA 96, Sections 11.2.1 to 11.2.3, require a service frequency of 6 months for listed hoods with fire-actuated water systems, mechanical or electrical detectors, actuators, and fire-actuated dampers. These hoods should be checked according to the manufacturers listed procedures and specific inspection requirements of applicable NFPA 96 Standards.

Many restaurant owners do not realize that water wash systems require service and maintenance beyond normal exhaust cleaning and fire-extinguishing systems maintenance. Water wash hoods are rather complex and will only function properly when all components work in conjunction with each other. When these systems are not checked regularly, they are prone to malfunction, particularly the dampers and wash nozzles.

This is probably one of the most overlooked areas in kitchen exhaust servicing.

Frequency of Service

NFPA 96, Section 11.2.1 requires that <u>water wash hoods</u> and <u>fire-extinguishing</u> <u>systems</u> be checked and tested every six months, to ensure that they continue to operate properly.

> *NFPA 96, Section 11.2.1*: Maintenance of the fire-extinguishing systems and listed exhaust hoods containing a constant or fire-activated water system that is listed to extinguish a fire in the grease removal devices, hood exhaust plenums, and exhaust ducts shall be made by properly trained, qualified, and certified person(s) acceptable to the authority having jurisdiction at least every 6 months.*

One of the major benefits of a listed water wash type hood (with dampers) is that it is designed to offer a degree of protection in case of a fire. However, if the components of the system are not maintained, especially the dampers and water spray nozzles, the systems operation will become suspect.

> *NFPA 96, Sections 11.2.2* and 11.2.3: All actuation and control components, including remote manual pull stations, mechanical and electrical devices, detectors, and actuators, shall be tested for proper operation during the inspection in accordance with the manufacturer's procedures. The specific inspection and maintenance requirements of the extinguishing system standards as well as the applicable installation and maintenance manuals for the listed system and service bulletins shall be followed.*

We have provided a sample form, which reviews the key points a service provider will check. Contact manufacturers for copies of their forms and locations of trained and authorized service providers.

Water Wash Service Check Points

The following is a list of components to be checked when a technician services the water wash hood:

- Time clock
- Cartridges
- Plenum
- Spray Nozzles
- Solvent Flow

- Drains
- Air Velocity
- Damper and Manual Control
- Detectors (Fenwal)
- Wash Time

Water Wash Forms

After Service Follow-up

The service technician is required to leave a dated Inspection Report and any brief comments, attached to the door of the control panel.

Quest CleanAir Inspection

NAME OF INSTALLATION: _____

LOCATION: _____

SERIAL NUMBER: _____ MODELS: _____ TOTAL LENGTH: _____

WE HAVE TODAY CHECKED YOUR QUEST CLEANAIR VENTILATOR AND REPORT THE FOLLOWING CONDITIONS

VENTILATOR FUNCTIONS		CHECK	COMMENTS	SERVICE REQUIRED
TIME CLOCK	CORRECT TIME			
	START [ ] WASH [ ]			
WASH TIME	TIMER SET FOR [ ] MIN			
CARTRIDGES				
PLENUM				
SPRAYS				
WASH PRESSURE	KG/M² [ ] PSI			
SOLVENT FLOW	DEMA [ ] PUMP			
WATER TEMP.	°C OR °F			
PLUMBING				
WATER SOLENOID(S)				
DRAIN(S)				
AIR VELOCITY	L/S [ ] FPM			
SOLVENT STOCK				

VENTILATOR FIRE CONTROLS: (IF EQUIPPED WITH EXTINGUISHER — BY CERTIFIED PERSONNEL ONLY)

	CHECK		
DAMPER MANUAL LEVER(S)	[ ]		
DAMPER(S) CLEAN & OPERATIONAL	[ ]		
DETECTORS CLEAN & OPERATIONAL	[ ]		
REMOTE ELECT. ACTUATOR(S)	[ ]		

FIRE EXTINGUISHER: (BY CERTIFIED PERSONNEL ONLY)

TANK PRESSURE		
INDICATOR LIGHT		
NOZZLES CLEAR [ ] LOCATION		
DETECTORS CLEAN [ ] LOCATION		
MECH. PULL ACCESSIBLE [ ] TEST		
AUTO. OPERATION TEST [ ]		
FUEL SHUT DOWN GAS [ ] ELECTRIC [ ]		

AUXILIARY EQUIPMENT

EXHAUST DUCTWORK	– WELDED	
	– ACCESS	
EXHAUST FAN	– ROTATION	
	– MOTOR	
	– BELT	
	– HOUSING	
MAKE-UP AIR	– BALANCE	
	– UNIT	

GENERAL CONDITIONS: _____

RECEIVED BY: _____ (Customer) SIGNED: _____

Nº 0035 DATE: _____

RUSSELL FOOD EQUIPMENT LIMITED
SERVICE DEPARTMENT

White copy - Head Office / Yellow copy - Customer / Pink copy - Branch Office

SAMPLE

Ultraviolet Hoods Maintenance

Ultra violet light bulbs are placed within the plenum directly behind removable extractors. As grease-laden air passes around the UV bulbs, usually arranged in a set of four or five, a chemical reaction takes place changing the grease to a fine white or gray powder. To oversimplify the process, the grease particles get "zapped."

These units come in canopy and galley hood design and some have water wash features.

Note: Behind the removable extractor there is an expanded metal screening device.

Staff Maintenance

The kitchen staff should carry out maintenance of the removable cartridges and metal "filter" during routine cleaning program. These pieces can be put through the dishwasher or the pot sink.

The UV lamps will accumulate dust from the chemical reaction process and need to be cleaned approximately every quarter (over heavy grease producing cooking the frequency will increase). As these bulbs give off a UV light (UV-C) that is dangerous, to the human eyes especially, the cabinet they are mounted in is locked and only the recognized maintenance personal have access.

The middle lightweight filter behind the cartridge

Looking up at the UV bulbs. Controls in the system will shut the bulbs off if the cartridges are removed

Recirculating (APCU) Maintenance

In the vast majority of cases where there is an Air Pollution Control Unit, a water wash hood by the same manufacturer will be installed. The technicians servicing one of these units will <u>not</u> necessarily service the other. See APCU in Chapter 4 Hoods.

APCUs must be maintained and be in compliance with other NFPA (or other fire bylaw) standards.

Recirculating Service Follow-up

Recirculating systems shall be installed and maintained in accordance with NFPA 96, Chapter 13 requirements. Each component shall comply with the corresponding chapters and sections of the NFPA 96 Standard.

Like fire-extinguishing system and water wash hood manufacturers, recirculating systems suppliers will provide a copy of the Service Follow-Up Report. This report and maintenance schedule is to be maintained in the control cabinet of the appliance.

Because of the combustible nature of the filtration mediums it cannot be stressed enough that these systems must be regularly maintained and deficiencies reported.

Prior to working on these systems, service personnel should contact the manufacturer and obtain written instructions on the safe handling of the components. In particular, the Electrostatic Precipitator (ESP), commonly called an Electronic Air Cleaner (EAC) is a sensitive item and must be handled accordingly.

A ventless fryer unit. Courtesy of Giles Industries.

The cleaning and maintenance schedule that is posted on a ventless fryer. Courtesy of Giles Industries.

Fire-Extinguishing Servicing

The following trades are involved in the continued maintenance of the fixed pipe fire-extinguishing system:

- System manufacturer
- System owner
- Service provider

Who is "Qualified" to Service?

NFPA 17A, Section 7.3.1 (2002 Edition): A trained person who has undergone the instructions necessary to perform the maintenance and recharge service reliably and has the applicable manufacturer's listed installation and maintenance manual and service bulletins shall service the wet chemical fire-extinguishing system 6 months apart as outlined in 7.3.2. (Annex A.7.3.1)

If the service technician is not "factory trained," the manufacturer generally disavows any responsibility for the performance of the system. The validity of this policy is controversial in many areas.

Fire-extinguishing system manufacturers have a policy of issuing periodic bulletins to their UL system installation and instructional manuals. If a bulletin is issued, then that amended document becomes an integral part of the instruction manual. Confirm with the manufacturer if any recent bulletins had been issued on the effected fire-extinguishing system.

Example of a fire-extinguishing system service tag

Frequency of Service

NFPA 96, Section 11.2 requires that all fixed fire-extinguishing systems shall be inspected and tested semiannually. As a part of the listing and to ensure proper operation of the system the factory prescribes specific test and inspection protocols to follow. These checkpoints and tests will be different depending on the model and manufacturer of the fire-extinguishing system.

Fusible Link Replacement Requirements

The fusible metal alloy sensing elements on fusible links and automatic sprinkler heads are sensitive to the heat and grease environment of the kitchen.

NFPA 96, Section 10.2 explains:

- Fusible links (including links on fire damper assemblies) shall be replaced at least semiannually, or more frequently if necessary where required by the manufacturer

- Automatic sprinkler heads that have become contaminated with grease shall be replaced semiannually. If after a qualified inspection the sprinkler heads show no sign of buildup, their use can be continued.

A fusible link assembly that was not fastened to the hood. It has fallen out and now stops the filters from being put in safely.

- There is a year date-stamp on the links. This year date does not limit when the link can be used. These devices have unlimited shelf life. The intent of year date is to require replacement of fusible links that have been installed for up to 1 year to be replaced.

- The stamped year of manufacture and date of installation shall be marked on the system inspection tag. The tag shall be signed or initialed by the installer and kept on premise (usually at or near the control head or manual pull).

- Other detection devices such as mechanical or electrical detectors shall be serviced or replaced in accordance with the manufacturer's recommendations

Fire-Extinguishing Check Points

Installation, inspection and test forms should indicate that checking and testing of the various components has taken place as outlined in the following generic checklist:

- Inspect tamper seals
- Verify hazard dimensions
- Remove and check/clean nozzles
- Ensure distribution piping is internally clear and clean by testing with pressurized air and factory approved cleanser as required
- Check nozzles – aimed properly
- Check detectors – in proper location
- Inspect cable lines and corner pulleys
- Inspect agent containers – Verify container hydrostatic test date
- Test actuation of system from detectors (no agent will be discharged)
- Verify mechanical operation of system
- Verify gas and/or electric shut-off
- Verify alarm connection (if applicable)
- Replace all fusible links
- Clean quartzoid links and/or thermostats
- Verify auxiliary contacts (example – pressure switch)
- Actuate remote manual release – verify operation
- Actuate local release – verify operation
- Reset system
- Install new tamper seals
- Install record tag

Any deficiencies must be noted on the Inspection Report. A report must be provided to the system owner.

Inspectors Note: Caution should be taken when accepting Service Checklists with only a few points covered. This is a standard tactic of the "fly-by-night" companies.

Non-Compliance Tags

When fire-extinguishing systems are found to be defective in any way, (such as serious component antiquation or wear) many jurisdictions require that the service technician attach a "Non-Compliance" certificate (tag) on the system and provide the owner and in some cases the AHJ with a report of these discrepancies for remedy.

> *New Change 2011 NFPA 96 11.1.6 Cooking equipment shall not be operated while its fire-extinguishing system or exhaust system is nonoperational or impaired.*

> *New Change 2011 NFPA 96 11.1.6.1 Where the fire-extinguishing system or exhaust system is nonoperational or impaired, the systems shall be tagged noncompliant, and the owners or the owner's representative shall be notified in writing of the impairment.*

> *NFPA 96, (2008 ed.) Section 11.2.8: Where required, certificates of inspection and maintenance shall be forwarded to the authority having jurisdiction.*

In spite of these requirements, there are many areas that allow a suppression system to be "red tagged" but continue to operate. For further details see Key Changes in Chapter 2, Codes.

Adding the two words "in writing" to the Standard will, hopefully motivate fire inspectors to require prompt reporting of non-operational or impaired suppression systems.

What is a "Red Tag" and what should a restaurant owner know?

Some suppression companies think that all they have to do is put a "red tag" (non-compliant tags) on the system and they have no liability. The practice of "red-tagging" suppression systems and what that actually means is very inconsistent across the country. This issue should be one of considerable importance to the fire inspector and insurance company.

Some states do not allow red tagging; instead, requiring an immediate repair for fire system impairments.

Where impairments are found it is advisable for the service company to send written notification by post/courier that provides proof of delivery.

What is the policy in your department?

It will be interesting to see if unscrupulous service providers consider just giving out red tags as providing notification "in writing."

Fire-Extinguishing Forms

The service provider will supply the owner with a maintenance report listing what was serviced along with any recommendations.[6]

Each manufacturer will have a prescribed set of inspection points. Consult the system installation and maintenance document (owner's manual).

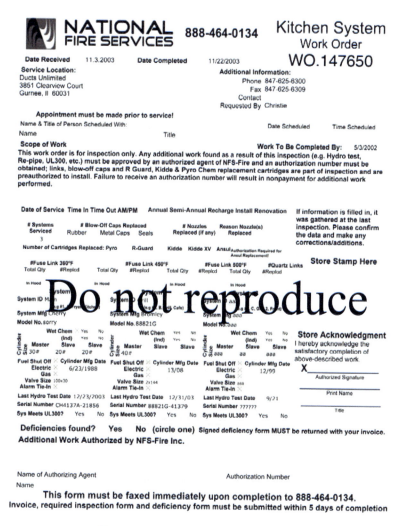

Courtesy of Facilitec Central LLC

---

[6] See NFPA 17A, Section 7.3.2.5.

Poor Servicing

During each 6-month service, the technician is required to conduct an extensive series of tests to ensure the system will function as designed. One of the most omitted services is conducting a trip-test of the detection system. A trip test will confirm that the detection cable moves freely through the EMT piping and that the gas shutoff will activate in the case of a trip. The piping is notorious for becoming plugged and freezing the cable. Oriental style cooking and high volume deep-frying are the most common sources of this sticky grease.

In general, the fire-extinguishing system is only as good as it's last service. If some component is found to be defective or in some way not compatible with the total system, then the service technician has a responsibility to repair it, clearly inform the owner of the system, and/or "red tag" it (put a non-compliant tag on the system). If the condition is extremely serious the technician may decide that the use of appliances must stop.

Typical poor service -- The fire-extinguishing service provider only changed the link, he did not clean the detector assembly, cable, or other parts of the system as required of service

A close-up of fusible link detection bracket and cable. Carbonized grease did not allow the cable to release and the system did not discharge.

The trip at the control head was never tightened (cocked) so the line was loose

An old dry chemical fire-extinguishing system located over a solid fuel charbroiler. The fusible link melted in the fire but the distribution piping was plugged from a previous discharge. Additionally the kitchen staff covered the nozzles with aluminum foil to keep them from getting dirty. This is a very poor practice because the foil can create a blockage for the distribution of the fire-extinguishing agent.

Contents of an Ansul nozzle after the system had tripped. After every discharge all nozzles must be removed and cleaned. Often (as in this case) the service provider will only come in and refill the tank and replace any broken links. The chemicals used in fire-extinguishing can crystallize once they dry. Therefore it is important to properly flush out the system per manufacturer's instructions. Courtesy of Don Reason.

Looking up into the duct entrance. The fusible link assembly is blocking the fire-extinguishing distribution nozzle.

Improperly installed/located piping and detector. Pipe required to be supported. The extinguishing service provider neglected to install the fusible link!

Servicing Portable Fire Extinguishers

The following are servicing requirements for system owners:

- Owner or representative should inspect portable monthly (See NFPA#10, 2010 Edition, 7.1)

- Persons performing maintenance shall be certified.

- Portables need to be maintained at least once a year (See NFPA#10, 2010 Edition, 7.3 *Maintenance*)

- Hydrostatic test required every 12 years

- 6-year internal inspection

- A placard identifying the use of the portable as a secondary backup to the automatic fire-extinguishing system needs to be conspicuously. (See NFPA 96, Section 10.2.2)

- Portable fire extinguishers shall be specifically listed and installed in cooking areas. (See NFPA 96 Section 10.10 *Portable Fire Extinguishers*, 1 through 5)

- Extinguishers shall use agents that saponify hot grease such as sodium bicarbonate and potassium bicarbonate dry chemical and potassium carbonate solutions

- Class B gas-type portables shall not be permitted in kitchen cooking areas

- Manufacturer's recommendations shall be followed

- Other fire extinguishers in the kitchen area shall be installed in accordance with NFPA 10

Facilitec-Central's plant where ABC portables are being filled.

Servicing Fire Dampers

The dampers and their fusible links or actuators become heavily coated with grease. They need cleaning and replacement on a regular basis.

Actuation components for the fire dampers must be inspected in accordance with the manufacturer's procedures. This will generally be every 6 months, unless under heavy use.

A certified person shall change the fusible links every 6 months. In the vast majority of case, these links are <u>not</u> being changed. This is not necessarily the responsibility of the fire suppression servicing company, as might be assumed.

The installer (the person who changes the link) needs to document the year on the link and the date of installation.

A terrible installation of a hood and duct. The ductwork is not welded but caulked with high-temp duct sealant (non-compliant) and the suppression system was not installed

Dates on fusible links -- The date stamp on the link does not limit their use. The links have unlimited shelf life, the date is to reference the date install (in writing). The environment in a kitchen hood or duct will adversely affect the links operation.

Kitchen Exhaust Cleaners

Introduction

The responsibility of the cleaner is to inspect for and remove combustible grease buildup from within the exhaust system. Cleaners are responsible to inform, in writing, the customer of areas of the exhaust system not cleaned or accessible for cleaning.

Conscienious cleaners additionally assist with fire prevention by providing reports of serious fire hazards relating to the exhaust system, such as:

- Non-compliant issues
- Lack of access
- Inferior construction and installation of exhaust systems
- Grease buildup outside the duct on extinguisher components and on the roof

Inspecting for Cleanliness

The primary focus of an "inspection for cleanliness" is to establish whether the volume of grease buildup warrants cleaning and to determine whether adequate access is available throughout the exhaust system. For further details see Key Changes in Chapter 2, Codes.

NFPA 96 states that the exhaust system shall be inspected for grease buildup by a properly trained, qualified, and certified (TQC) ~~company or~~ person(s) acceptable to the authority having jurisdiction.

> *11.4 Inspection of Grease Buildup. The entire exhaust system shall be inspected for grease buildup by a properly trained, qualified and certified ~~company or~~ person(s) acceptable to the authority having jurisdiction and in accordance with Table 11.4.*

This new standard removes the word "company." The substantiation was, there needs to be a properly trained, qualified and certified (TQC) <u>person</u> doing the work. In many cases large companies are getting "certified" and then declaring that all their people are therefore "trained, qualified and certified" when they are not.[7]

Unfortunately this change clouds the "qualifications" which are generally considered to be adequate insurance and business license, which are held by a <u>company</u>, not necessarily an individual.

What is your department's policy toward "licensing/recognizing" (holding responsible) any of these services required by commercial kitchen fire safety devices?

---

[7] Phil Ackland Certification (PAC) is very specific that there must be <u>at least one</u> certified individual on the cleaning or inspecting crew. If a cleaning company were to claim to be PAC and not have at least one individual on the job who is PAC, then their company qualification is void.

NFPA 96 Table 11.4 Schedule of Inspection for Grease Buildup

Type or Volume of Cooking	Frequency
Systems serving solid fuel cooking operations	Monthly
Systems serving high-volume cooking operations such as 24-hour cooking, charbroiling or wok cooking	Quarterly
System serving moderate-volume cooking operations	Semiannually
Systems serving low-volume cooking operations, such as churches, day camps, seasonal businesses, or senior centers	Annually

Exhaust Cleaner's Responsibilities

When grease is found in the exhaust system at a depth 2000 microns (0.078 in.) it needs to be removed. Hood and duct surfaces should be cleaned to a minimum of 50 microns (0.002 in.). NFPA adopted a depth gauge to provide a means of measuring grease residue depth.[8]

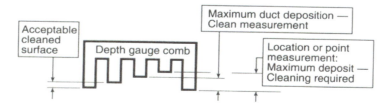

Drawing of a Depth gauge comb used for determining grease buildup in exhaust system

NFPA 96, Section 11.6.1 continues by stating that if the system is contaminated with grease deposits (residues) then it should be cleaned by a trained, qualified, and certified (TQC) individual:

- The entire system cleaned

- Switches and controls must be locked out

- No flammable solvents are to be used to cleaning

- All access panels, dampers, and other controls must be returned to their operational state

- The exhaust system shall not be coated with powder after cleaning

Note: Most professional TQC exhaust cleaners will install access panels because it assists them in removal of all grease residues throughout the entire system.

Examples of dirty and clean ductwork

---

[8] NFPA 96, Sections 11.4 and Annex A.

Certification of Exhaust Cleaners

Phil Ackland Certification Protocol™

Important Note: Phil Ackland, the author of this manual, is no longer associated with Phil Ackland Training LLC (PAT) and the training and certification of exhaust cleaners. We do continue to support (PAT) efforts to train and certify commercial kitchen exhaust cleaners, but have no official affiliation.

This certification provides guidelines for commercial kitchen exhaust cleaning companies and their Crew Leaders (the individual on the job site at the time of the cleaning or responsible for inspecting the system immediately after cleaning) and the Authority Having Jurisdiction (AHJ) to establish a consistent and recordable set of Competencies for commercial kitchen exhaust cleaners. In 1998, to improve commercial kitchen fire safety, NFPA 96 approved the proposal that restaurant exhaust systems be inspected and cleaned:

> *New NFPA 96 (2011 ed) 11.6.1 Upon inspection, if the exhaust system is found to be contaminated with deposits from grease-laden vapors, the contaminated portions of the exhaust system shall be cleaned <u>by a properly trained, qualified, and certified person(s) acceptable to the authority having jurisdiction.</u>*

Since that time a growing number of States, Provinces and other jurisdictions are requiring exhaust system cleaning certification as proof of competency to comply with code requirements. For further details see Key Changes in Chapter 2, Codes.

Phil Ackland Company Qualifications (PA/CQ)[9] and Crew Leader Certification (PAC) herein referred to as PA/CQ and PAC, was created to provide guidelines for the restaurant industry, Authority Having Jurisdiction and exhaust cleaners. They establish a consistent and measurable Standard of Care provided by these service companies and individuals, thereby fulfilling the requirements of NFPA standards involving commercial exhaust cleaners.

If a company sends out Crew Leaders who are not PAC, the company's certification is <u>void</u>.[10]

PA/CQ and PAC provides practical definitions of what trained, qualified and certified measurement should be when a company or person is seeking to meet the benchmark of ".....acceptable to the Authority Having Jurisdiction."

Purpose

PA/CQ and PAC provides a consistent set of minimum measurements and qualifications for those who inspect and clean commercial exhaust systems.

The primary goals of PA/CQ and PAC are:

- Qualify the Company (legal entity doing business)

- Train and Certify the Crew Leader (that individual who is on the job site at the time of the cleaning, who is responsible for the companies actions)

- Ensure that a Crew Leader has a <u>minimum</u> level of training and has an understanding of the fire and mechanical codes related to cleaning of commercial kitchen systems.

- Ensure that companies and Crew Leaders have a formal policy of providing a written *After Service Follow-Up Report* to customers. This follow-up report will primarily inform the customer if there are areas of the exhaust systems that could not be cleaned and why this was so. The report may have more information, such as visible deficiencies that are within the Standard of Care of an exhaust cleaner.

- Elevate professionalism of persons and companies performing exhaust system cleaning in general

---

[9] The name *Phil Ackland Company Qualifications* and *Phil Ackland Certification* are meant to be only <u>temporary</u> names until the Protocol is adopted by the appropriate governing jurisdictions.

[10] For a copy of the PAC Pledge, see Articles and Forms on http://www.philackland.com/

The establishment of a Standard of Care for acceptable practices will provide end users, AHJ's, insurance agencies etc. a benchmark to judge whether the performance (service) of a cleaning company or individual meets the requirements as per the code.

Cleaners Certification Details

The following details provide guidance on certifying kitchen hood and duct cleaning contractors. Thus ensuring that these kitchen exhaust cleaners fulfill the necessary steps to gain certification.

PA/CQ and PAC is a two step process:

1. Qualification of the exhaust cleaning Company (the PA/CQ portion)

2. Training and Certification of exhaust cleaning Crew Leaders (achieving the PAC portion)

The process of PA/CQ and PAC can be accomplished by correspondence or attending an authorized training course.

Exhaust Cleaner After Service Follow-up Reporting

It is the responsibility of the exhaust cleaner to inform the restaurant owner, in writing (via a label), of areas not cleaned. It is also good practice for the exhaust cleaner to inform the restaurant of areas of inaccessibility (where grease either cannot be inspected or removed). Ultimately it is the restaurant owner's responsibility for the inspection and cleaning of the exhaust system, including the provision of access panels, unless that responsibility has been transferred in written form to another party.[11]

All too often exhaust systems are not cleaned for years. Massive amounts of grease will accumulate. Photo courtesy of Chris Gibson.

> *NFPA 96, Section 11.6.13: When an exhaust cleaning company is used, a certificate showing the name of the servicing company, the name of the person performing the work, and the date of inspection or cleaning shall be maintained on the premises.*

> *11.6.14 After cleaning or inspection is completed, the exhaust cleaning company and the person performing the work at the location shall provide the owner of the system with a written report that also specifies areas that were inaccessible or not cleaned.*

> *11.6.15 Where required, certificates of inspection and cleaning and reports of areas not cleaned shall be submitted to the authority having jurisdiction.*

Beware of service companies that issue certificates that imply that they are "certified" to NFPA standards. The National Fire Protection Association (NFPA) does <u>not</u> certify any contractor or their personnel or processes. Any exhaust cleaning contract should state that the cleaning is in accordance with the procedures specified in the NFPA 96 Standard.

Cleaning Forms

Cleaning Certificate of Performance

NFPA 96 requires a Certificate of Performance be maintained on the premise. Usually it is posted on or near the hood. The Certificate of Performance should state the date the system was cleaned and expiration date (date it is due to be cleaned again).

The Certificate must state the 'Standard' to which the system was cleaned and if any areas were <u>not</u> cleaned, the reason why – reported <u>In Writing!</u>

---

[11] See NFPA 96, Section 4.1.5.

If there are serious inaccessible areas a trained, qualified and certified company will send the system owner notification of the deficiency in an *After Service Follow-Up Report*.

Exhaust Cleaning Performance Form

The Cleaner Performance Form outlines the various standards and conditions, which apply to cleaning exhaust systems. Several of the requirements reference NPFA 96. Other references cover restaurant equipment, property safety or provide guidelines for the handling of wastes created by the cleaning process.

This form will remove confusion regarding what is expected of the contractor and will protect the system owner from shoddy workmanship.

After Service Follow-Up Report

Reporting on the condition of the exhaust system is one of the greatest services an exhaust cleaner can provide. Certified exhaust cleaners receive training to identify most of the serious problems in exhaust systems.

After the cleaning job a *Certificate of Performance* and *After Service Follow-Up Report* summarize the condition and cleanliness of the system.

The After Service Follow-up Report can be used in two ways; by the exhaust cleaning company that has just completed the job, <u>or</u> by an inspector who is checking the work of the cleaner.

For the exhaust cleaner the report provides an excellent opportunity to inform the customer of the condition of the exhaust system.

This report outlines:

- Inaccessible areas

- The ability of the fan to be tipped

- The conditions of all the various components of the system

- Any other exhaust problems

A fire suppression distribution nozzle.

Exhaust Cleaners and the Fire-Extinguishing System

Only trained fire-extinguishing service personnel are allowed to work on the fire-extinguishing system. Exhaust cleaners are generally not qualified.

The fire-extinguishing system is to remain operational during cleaning, except where serviced by properly trained and qualified persons.

Many fusible links and/or assemblies are made of aluminum. Most cleaning chemicals used by exhaust cleaners corrode aluminum. NFPA 96 states that cleaning chemicals are not to be applied to the fusible links or other detection devices. This makes it difficult to clean around these components.

It is the responsibility of the fire-extinguishing service company and the restaurant owner to ensure the fusible links, nozzles, and other extinguishing components are clean.

Exhaust cleaners are <u>not</u> responsible to clean fire-extinguishing detection (links) components.[12] However, it is a good practice for cleaners to inform the restaurant if there is serious grease buildup on the links, nozzles or other parts of the fire-extinguishing system.

---

[12] See NFPA 96, Section 11.6.7.

Chapter Eight - Inspections

Phil showing participants the fire-extinguishing system in the
Fire Inspector Course

Inspections

Pre-Construction Inspections

Introduction

As commercial cooking operations become more complex, the need for knowledge and understanding of kitchen ventilation systems increases. The challenge for Building and Fire Inspectors is to stay current with the various components and ensure that these components are compatible when joined together in a complete system.

This chapter provides information to review projects; general information that AHJ officials should be aware of when beginning the review work on a newly submitted project.

This chapter is directed primarily to Building and Fire Inspectors. The information will also be valuable to those trades that must work with these AHJ's.

The design/installation phase is the best time to ensure that these systems are going to work properly. At this point the installation of access, balanced fire extinguisher coverage[1], clearances, tippable fans, and proper air balancing, etc. can be more easily confirmed. After the exhaust system is up and running, repairs and upgrades are that much more difficult.

The Planning Flow

Developers and those involved in supplying and installing the various components should confirm which Standards and Codes they must operate under and what (if any) variances and exceptions are acceptable to the AHJ.

Information needs to be well organized, accurate and complete.

Editorial Comment: Communications

One of the obstacles to maximize performance is that the various disciplines, designers, engineers and the AHJ community fail to communicate with each other except through the documents they are responsible for.

Misunderstandings can be avoided if all parties are talking the same language, understanding the drawings, specifications and communicating in general.

Part of the challenge for the AHJ is to understand the role of designers and engineers; be familiar with the appropriate codes, standards, testing, products and interaction between the equipment; and be comfortable signing off on the CKV system. This book will assist the AHJ in understanding and appreciating the importance of the interrelationship between all these components.

Important Note: It is a practice of many jurisdictions that the Fire Department Inspectors be involved in the approval of any plans with the Building Department. This practice helps assure the overall effectiveness of the system.

An inspector checking the access panels

---

[1] All appliances are covered according to the manufacturer's instructions and UL 300.

Building and Ventilation Component Construction References

Codes & Standards

Confirm the editions of whatever Codes and Standards are being used on the jobsite. Ensure that all parties are on the same page regarding the Codes.

On multi-tenant sites there is a particular need for concerted cooperation of design, installation, operation, and maintenance responsibilities by tenants and by the building owner.

Handbooks Available For Reference:[2]

- ASHRAE HANDBOOK
- ETL
- NFPA HANDBOOK – Sections 11 and 12
- NSF INTERNATIONAL
- PG&E Design Guides I and II
- SMACNA
- UL and ULC

Websites and The Internet

The Internet provides the ability to communicate plans and revisions. There are many opportunities to access drawings, shop drawings, details, specifications and manufacturer cut sheets.

Architects and engineers can make current drawings and modifications available in a variety of ways; such as: projects with dedicated websites to .ftp sites.

Documents are under constant revision due to errors being corrected, additional information being added, revisions being requested by the owner and many other legitimate reasons. Always note the version of a document and its current date for record purposes.

Maintain records of various document revisions and dates for future reference.

Areas and Components That Require Design and Code Compliance

- Standards
- Hoods
- List of acceptable design practices
- Exhaust flow rates
- Grease filters
- Ductwork
- Types of exhaust fans
- Types of makeup air fans
- Makeup air systems
- Testing and balancing
- Fire-extinguishing system equipment

---

[2] For more information see http://www.philackland.com/docs/appendix.pdf

Preliminary Plan Review

Obtain good documentation, also referred to as "deliverables" from the submitter.

Confirm all plans or specification details.

Require that architects, engineers, designers, foodservice consultants and owners discuss preliminary design plans. This step can be invaluable to all parties.

Permit Submittal Essentials

The following should be required for a permit:

- Clearly reproducible drawings
- A detailed set of specifications
- Full set of manufacturers cut sheets
- Manufacturer shop drawings as necessary
- Supporting architectural documents
- Supporting mechanical, electrical and HVAC documents

DO NOT accept block plans, preliminary sketches or incomplete documents except for preliminary discussion purposes. Require all parties to define, in writing, precisely what they are going to do or supply; and the specifications of these products or services.

List of Good Design Practices

This list of design practices is from ASHRAE's Technical Committee for Kitchen Ventilation, TC-5.10. The committee is responsible for Chapter 33 in the 2011 ASHRAE HANDBOOK. While these recommendations are not mandatory, implementation by a submitter may indicate that they are keeping up with the latest best practices.

Note: Not all comments apply to all conditions.

- Increased front hood overhang to 30.5 cm (12 in.) (Note that this is more than the IMC 15.2 cm [6 in.] minimum requirement)
- Push equipment back to minimize the rear gap between equipment and back of the hood
- Add a rear seal at cooking equipment (e.g. shelf below cooking height)
- Minimize hood mounting height to 2 m (6 ft – 6 in.) above finished floor
- Use back shelf or proximity style hoods when practical
- Employ side or end panels or end walls
- When practical, locate heavy duty broilers toward the middle of hood
- When practical, locate higher light duty ovens at ends
- Do not waste hood space over non-cooking areas (unless future appliances planned)
- Introduce makeup air at low velocity
- Do not locate 4 way ceiling makeup air diffusers closer than 3 m (10 ft) from hood
- Use perforated or slot diffusers in lieu of 4 way units

Mesh aluminum filters are too close to the heat of the flue gas exhaust of the salamander. Why do people insist on wrapping the pipes with aluminum foil?

Renovating Pre-used Ventilation Components

Used ventilation equipment must be closely inspected. Ask the following questions:

- Is it in good condition?

- Does it meet current local codes?

- Does it meet the application? (e.g.) Attempting to use a non-compliant Type II hood where the cooking application requires a Type I hood.

- In the case of an existing operation, is the submitter trying to "grandfather" a used piece of equipment purchased for the sole purpose of passing it off as existing?

- Are all penetrations from previous fire-extinguishing system piping and conduit properly sealed?

- Does the hole in the hood from the previous duct match up with the new duct?

Documents – Final Foodservice Drawings

The following is a list of documents/deliverables.

1. Require good drawings with the following information:

    a. Minimum 6.4 mm (0.25 in.) scale foodservice equipment plan containing:

        i. Item numbers

        ii. Corresponding equipment schedule

        iii. Related building walls, columns, doorways, etc.

        iv. Dimensioning

2. Minimum 12.7 mm (0.5 in.) scale elevations of equipment

    a. Item numbers keyed to plan and schedule

    b. Minimum 3.8 cm (1.5 in.) scale cross sections at:

        i. Exhaust hoods/cooking lineups

        ii. Low ceiling conditions

        iii. Odd building situations such as slanted rooflines, etc.

3. Minimum 6.4 mm (0.25 in.) scale mechanical plan

    a. Dimensioned "rough-in plan"

    b. Schedule of symbols

    c. Schedule of equipment connections defining:

        i. Gas, hot and cold water, closed waste, steam

        ii. Height above floor for each

        iii. Remarks indicating "tee-offs" to adjoining equipment

        iv. Floor drains, floor sinks properly located for cleaning/maintenance purposes

        v. Area floor drains

        vi. Trench drains/floor troughs if applicable

        vii. Grease interceptors if required per local code either inside or outside the building

        viii. Special requirements

4. Minimum 6.4 mm (0.25 in.) scale electrical plan

    a. Dimensioned "rough-in plan"

    b.   Schedule of symbols

    c.   Schedule of equipment requirements defining:

        i.   Junction box locations

        ii.   Plug-in outlet locations

        iii.   Voltage designations

        iv.   Amperage requirements

        v.   Height above floor for each

    d.   Special requirements such as:

Pop rivets holding the duct to the hood

        i.   Conduit for beverage or refrigeration lines

        ii.   Sleeves in walls or floors for above

    e.   Location of distribution panels serving equipment

5.   Minimum 6.4 mm (0.25 in.) scale CKV kitchen exhaust requirements

    a.   Duct exhaust collar sizes for each hood

    b.   Dimensioned location of each duct

    c.   CFM (Cubic Feet per Minute) requirements

    d.   S.P. (Static Pressure) at each hood/canopy

    e.   Note that this information may be included on plumbing or electric

    f.   Control panel for a water wash CKV system if used

    g.   Access panel locations, rating, gasket, fasteners and fire rated penetrations

6.   Shop Drawings

    a.   Specially fabricated equipment require shop drawings, such as:

        i.   CKV exhaust hoods

        ii.   Water wash systems

        iii.   Variable speed CKV systems

        iv.   Pollution control systems

        v.   Utility distribution systems

Note: All of the above drawings form the basis for well executed architectural and engineering documents that provide proper information to co-ordinate the project.

A foodservice consultant, dealer or a combination of the two may provide the specific food service drawings referred to above.

Possible CKV Complexities

Modern commercial kitchen ventilation systems can be very complex particularly those housed in the same room. Ensure that sufficient data has been provided on any of these issues prior to allowing them to be included in the design of the ventilation system.

- Unanticipated elbows/turns in a duct that add static pressure

- Variable air (fan) speed controls

- New emerging technologies (UV and Ceiling systems)

- Unlisted hoods

- Multiple hood or canopy styles
- Numerous filtration methods
- Different/specific ventilation and cooking (foods and appliance) applications
- Mixed makeup air capacities and delivery designs
- Unusually long duct runs

Specifications

1. Require a well written and complete set of specifications

   a. Larger projects will include AIA (American Institute of Architects) formatted bid documents

      i. Section 11-400 of these documents will include foodservice

      ii. Section 23-3800 contains ventilation hoods

      iii. Section 23-7400 contains packaged HVAC equipment

      iv. Section 23-7500 contains custom packaged outdoor HVAC

      v. Section 23-7600 contains Evaporative Air Cooling equipment

   b. Always ask about the latest revision date (unless a representative from the architect, engineer or dealer is visiting with deliverables, assume the documents have already been revised)

      i. Manufacturer should be identified

      ii. Model number specified

      iii. Electrical, gas or steam requirements

      iv. Included options

2. Do not accept a one line list of items

Equipment Cut or Specification Sheets

1. Detailed cut sheets from manufacturers

2. Verify that the cut sheets match the schedules and specifications

3. Ask for an explanation if something does not match

Poorly installed suppression blocks the installation of the filters.

Shop Drawings

Commercial kitchens often require specially fabricated equipment such as:

1. Exhaust hoods

   a. Listed or unlisted hood canopy – Style

   b. Backshelf (proximity or galley) or Passover

   c. Type I style for grease producing equipment

   d. Filter type (some newer dual-stage types require a higher static pressure)

   e. Water wash

   f. Ultra Violet

   g. Other

h. Type II for humidity and non-grease producing equipment

2. Integration of fire-extinguishing system

a. Locate fire-extinguishing system cabinet

b. Cabinet may be integral with hood

c. Cabinet may be remote on wall or above ceiling

d. Be sure fire-extinguishing system is designed for relocation of equipment below the hood in existing kitchens being remodeled

3. Pollution control system (Air Purification Units)

a. Require space and frequent maintenance access

b. Is exit air being sent outside or being returned inside the building?

4. Utility Distribution Systems (referred to as a UDS)

Supporting Architectural and MEP Documents

The documents above refer mainly to the foodservices areas. All of the information must be supported by architectural and MEP (mechanical/electrical/plumbing), HVAC, civil, structural, etc. drawings, that go to makeup the documents to complete a building.

Pre-Occupancy Inspections

Pre-occupancy inspections are a challenge for the building inspector, the environmental health specialist and the fire safety official. However, it is also a challenge for the property owner, general contractor, architect and engineers. All must endeavor to meet local codes.

A duct installed next to a window. This is a vinyl sided building and safe fan access is impossible

It is important for the AHJ inspector to understand that architects and engineers are often employing much more up-to-date codes than what is being enforced at the local level. This is due to the normally long time it takes for local jurisdictions to adopt recently passed national codes. Often local jurisdictions are working with codes that have been updated several years ago at the national level but have not yet been adopted in their state, county or municipality. This can make for difficulties in the approval process unless the architectural side has a good working relationship with the inspector side. Another major reason to meet and discuss preliminary plans.

This is also the best time to make minor corrections to the ventilation to ensure its highest possible efficiency. Proper operation of a CKV system can be influenced by very minor adjustments in makeup air, fan speed and cross drafts.

With respect to the CKV systems difficult problems develop when there are:

- Poor installations by a contractor

- Leaks in welded ductwork

- Lack of access in the duct or fan

- Unsafe work surfaces

- Incorrect equipment placement

- Relocation of cooking equipment

- Lack of sufficient overhang

Prior to Occupancy Permit

Confirm that the ventilation is balanced. A major fault of the test and balance contractor is attempting to do the T&B before the cooking equipment and the exhaust system is fully operational. In order to have a good T&B, the cooking equipment must be turned on and hot to create a realistic thermal plume.

- Confirm that the fire-extinguishing system is fully operational and properly located over specific appliances

- Review written proof of operation of any engineered exhaust or fire-extinguishing system equipment

- Confirm that the exhaust system is clean and mechanically functioning as designed

Pre-Operational Inspection Checklist

The following are areas of greatest concern, in specific situations or specialty applications outside consultants. <u>Prior</u> to the ceilings and other interior paneling being installed, check the following:

Hoods

- All cooking equipment producing smoke or grease-laden vapors is under a Type I hood complying with NFPA 96

- Proof that a maintenance contract is in place for all "engineered systems" from a service company qualified for maintenance by the manufacturer is provided to the City prior to a request for occupancy

- Minimum clearances around the hood

- Space between deep fat fryers and surface flames from adjacent equipment is adequate

- All sources of fuel to all appliances will shut off upon fire-extinguishing system activation

- The makeup air is interlocked with the cooking exhaust system

- The wall behind cooking equipment is of fire proof construction

- Whenever the cooking equipment is turned on, the exhaust system shall be operating

- Start-up sequence will be as follows, with shutdown in reverse order:

    o Exhaust fan

    o Makeup air fan

    o Direct-fired makeup air heater

    o Cooking equipment

- All lights under the hood will be listed for under hood use

Because the pop rivets leaked, they covered the hood to duct connection with duct tape. Please note this is a really good quality duct tape, so that's ok then?

Fire-Extinguishing System

- The wet chemical fire-extinguishing system complies with NFPA 96, 17A and UL300 or ULC/ORD 1254.6 or UL197. The water sprinkler system complies with UL199E.

- The manual activation of the fire-extinguishing system is located in the egress path, in a familiar location for kitchen staff to use (e.g. near the cooking equipment), and is greater than or equal to 106.7 cm (42 in.) and less than or equal to 152.4 cm (60 in.) above the floor

- Does the building have a fire alarm system?

- If yes, does the kitchen fire-extinguishing system activate the building's fire alarm and annunciates as a separate zone (and annunciates separately from other kitchen fire-extinguishing system(s) that are in different areas)?

- Require a "dry" trip test, including blowing pressurized nitrogen through the distribution piping to ensure there are no obstructions[3]

- Require that all nozzles be removed by the servicing company to see if the internal filters are clean and clear

NFPA 17A Requirements of Fire-Extinguishing System Installation and Servicing

NFPA 17A, Section 6.1* Specifications (2002 Edition). Specifications for wet chemical fire-extinguishing systems shall be drawn up with care under the supervision of a trained person and with the advice of the authority having jurisdiction.

6.2* Review and Certification. Design and installation of systems shall be performed only by persons properly trained and qualified to design and/or install the specific system being provided. The installer shall provide certification to the authority having jurisdiction that the installation is in complete agreement with the terms of the listing and the manufacturer's instructions and/or approved design.

For further details see Chapter *Fire Extinguishers, Fire Extinguisher Installation and Management Responsibilities.*

Ducts

- Exhaust ducts are welded steel and liquidtight

- Exterior portions of ductwork and supports are protected with one of the following:

  o Non-corrosive stainless steel

  o Painted or weather-protection coating

- All ducts lead as directly as practical to the exterior of the building

- Ducts for a solid fuel appliance hoods are not combined with ducts for gas or other types of fuel. They must be separate with their own exhaust fan.

- Ducts from different fire compartments (fire rated separation areas of the building) are not combined into a single duct or single enclosure

- Ducts are not combined with any other building ventilation or exhaust system

- Shaft construction complies with defined Code requirements as either: combustible, limited-combustible or noncombustible

- Minimum clearance between the shaft and the duct is adequate (NFPA 4.2.3.1 or 4.2.3.2)

- Minimum clearance from ductwork and associated equipment where there is no shaft is adequate (457 mm/18 in.)

- What is the fire-resistance rating of the duct's shaft?

- At point of penetration (wall or roof), is there proper fire rated construction?

- Are ducts installed to Code requirements?

- Are there sufficient access panels in the ductwork?

- Are access panels properly rated?

- Will there be properly rated fire doors to gain access to any openings (access) in the duct?

- Where ductwork is connected to both sides of an exhaust fan, is there access at a minimum of 91.4 cm (3 ft) on each side of the fan?

---

[3] CO_2 can not be used as it will introduce moisture into the piping and promote rust or scaling

Editorial Comment - Testing the Welding Integrity in New Ductwork

Pressure testing of the exhaust duct during construction can insure a liquidtight duct system. In spite of welder's claims as to their expertise, most ductwork tested using pressure testing will find several leaks.

Fans

- Wall exhaust termination is greater than or equal to 3 m (10 ft) from property lines, combustible construction, grade, and from openings below

- The termination is greater than or equal to 9.9 m (32 ft – 6 in.) from openings above and will be accessible for maintenance

- The exhaust is greater than or equal to 3 m (10 ft) from any air intake (and greater than or equal to 9.9 m (32 ft – 6 in.) from openings above) and ends outside the building

- Fan support assembly is noncombustible

- Fans have been chosen so that their noise levels are in compliance with the local Noise Control By-laws

- Safe work area around the fan

- A hinge kit on an upblast fan or access into a utility fan

- Confirm that the roofing material around the duct/fan housing is secure and clearance issues are resolved

- Roof grease protection is in place

An inspector viewing a utility set fan

Start-up and Installation

Forms

The following are samples of forms from a fire-extinguishing system and water wash hood manufacturer.

In most cases it is a good practice to require the property owner have a signed service contract with a recognized and/certified service contractor.[4]

This System Installation Certificate is a generic example used to confirm that the fire-extinguishing system's components are fully operational.

Inspectors should require a copy of this certificate/form be maintained on the premise.

*Ensure approved fire and smoke
detectors are in place.*

---

[4] See Chapter 10, Service Providers.

VENTILATOR START-UP INSPECTION REPORT

Note: This Start-Up Report Used For Ventilators with C-3000 Series Control Cabinets.
One Report Must Be Completed For Each Control Cabinet.

Job Name _____   Gaylord Manufacturer _____

Address _____

City/State _____   Zip _____

EXHAUST FAN

1. Exhaust fan brand name _____ Model # _____
2. Total number of exhaust fans _____
3. Exhaust fan discharge _____ Vertical _____ Horizontal _____ Downward
4. Screen over discharge _____ Yes _____ No
5. Discharge away from air intake _____ Yes _____ No
6. Discharge free from obstructions _____ Yes _____ No
7. Discharge has weather cap _____ Yes _____ No
8. Ducts grease and watertight _____ Yes _____ No
9. Kitchen make-up air supply is turned on _____ Yes _____ No
10. Location of kitchen make-up air is _____ Good _____ Fair _____ Poor
11. Amount of kitchen make-up air is _____ Good _____ Fair _____ Poor

AIR READINGS:

Start ventilator and take air readings. Note: Exhaust to be recorded in feet per minute (FPM).
Supply reading, if MA Series ventilator, to be recorded in FPM.

Make and model of air meter used: _____

ITEM NO.									
VENT MODEL #									
AIR READING	EXHAUST VELOCITIES	CUSTOM AIR EXHAUST VELOCITIES	MAKE-UP AIR VELOCITIES	EXHAUST VELOCITIES	CUSTOM AIR EXHAUST VELOCITIES	MAKE-UP AIR VELOCITIES	EXHAUST VELOCITIES	CUSTOM AIR EXHAUST VELOCITIES	MAKE-UP AIR VELOCITIES
1.									
2.									
3.									
TOTAL									
AVERAGE									

NOTE: If ventilators being checked are "GX" Series, "Cleaning System" and "Fire System" sections are not to be completed. Exception: If "GX" Series ventilators are equipped with optional electrically operated dampers, perform "Fire System Damper Test" #1.

CLEANING SYSTEM:

1. Model of Control Cabinet _____
2. Push "START FAN" on Control Cabinet. Did exhaust fan turn on? _____ Yes _____ No
3. Push "START WASH" on Control Cabinet. Check the following:

A. Exhaust fan shut off _____ Yes _____ No   F. Water pressure _____ PSI

B. Water turned on _____ Yes _____ No   G. Water temperature _____

C. All nozzles spraying _____ Yes _____ No   H. Any ventilator leaks _____ Yes _____ No

D. Detergent pump operating _____ Yes _____ No   I. Drains free and clear _____ Yes _____ No

E. Length of cleaning cycle _____ minutes   J. Brand of detergent used _____

FIRE SYSTEM:

CAUTION: Before any fire tests are performed, check with building superintendent to see if Gaylord fire control is tied into building alarm, monitoring system and/or Fire Department.

DAMPER TEST *(NOT REQUIRED FOR RGF SERIES.)*

With ventilator on, trip damper control switch. The following should occur: (This must be done for each damper control switch in the system)

1. Exhaust fan shut off _____ Yes _____ No
2. Damper of ventilator closed tightly against lower hot water line _____ Yes _____ No

FIRE SWITCH TEST

On fire switch control flip toggle switch to the "ALARM or TEST" position. The following should occur:

1. Water spray turned on _____ Yes _____ No
2. Damper remained open _____ Yes _____ No
3. Fan remained on (or turned on) _____ Yes _____ No

NOTE: Water will continue to run for 5 min. after the toggle switch has been flipped back to the normal position. The water may be shut off prior to the end of the 5 min. cool down cycle by pushing the "EMERG STOP ONLY" button on the command center.

THERMOSTAT TEST

With the ventilator on, open electrical compartment on Control Cabinet and push the "Fire Test Switch". The following should occur:

1. Dampers on ventilator closed _____ Yes _____ No   *(Except RGF Series)*
2. Water turned on _____ Yes _____ No
3. Exhaust fan shut off _____ Yes _____ No

NOTE: Water will continue to run for 5 min. after the switch has been pushed. The water may be shut off prior to the end of the 5 min. cool down cycle by pushing the "EMERG STOP ONLY" button on the command center.

OPTIONAL EQUIPMENT:

1. Is ventilator equipped with The Gaylord Heat Reclaim Unit (HRU) _____ Yes _____ No If yes, HRU Start-Up form #HRUSU-888 to be completed.

2. Is ventilator equipped with The Gaylord "Quencher" Fire Protection System _____ Yes _____ No. If yes, Certification/Inspection Report Form #QUCIR-1088 to be completed.

Personnel provided with ventilator technical manual _____ Yes _____ No

Inspection Witnessed By _____

Gaylord Representative _____   Date _____

Comments: _____

_____

_____

_____

DISTRIBUTION: WHITE — Gaylord Industries, Inc. YELLOW — Customer PINK — Dealer GOLDENROD — Sales Litho U.S.A.

FORM -SUR-1088   GAYLORD INDUSTRIES, INC., P.O. Box 1149, 10900 S.W. Avery St., Tualatin, OR 97062-1149, 1-503-691-2010
A SUBSIDIARY OF GAYLORD INTERNATIONAL, INC.

Example of a water wash installation form

Post Operational Inspections

Introduction

A large number of existing exhaust systems are not up to current Fire Codes. Many of these older systems pose "Life-Safety" hazards, as defined by both the IMC and NFPA.

Regularly scheduled kitchen exhaust system inspections provide valuable findings.

The challenge for the fire inspector is to determine which (if any) of these deficiencies are serious enough to require modification. Even though the ventilation system is judged on the Code in force at the time of installation, certain improvements are required to ensure, primarily, that the grease can be removed from the system.

In particular:

- The need for additional access into the duct or fan for grease removal

- Proper tipping of the fan so the underside and duct can be accessed

- Safe working surfaces

All of which are often not originally installed.

Inspectors should be able to assess, and report on, the degree of grease contamination and other possible common deficiencies of kitchen exhaust systems.

A thorough understanding of local Fire and Building Codes is necessary to be able to properly assess kitchen exhaust systems. It is highly recommended that inspectors acquire copies of all Codes or Standards enforced in their jurisdiction.

Important Note: This Manual provides a guide that Building and Fire Inspectors, and/or service-oriented personnel can use to identify some of the more obvious, potential hazards in commercial kitchen exhaust systems. **Not all situations are covered.**

The grease residues in this exhaust duct are so thick; it is possible they have rendered the fire-extinguishing system inoperable

Grease overflowing the containment box and severely damaging the roof surface. Yes, that is a dead bird

Filters are installed the wrong direction   *A masking-taped access panel*

Two examples of non-compliant mesh type filters

Improper clearances to combustibles   *Filters installed incorrectly – baffles need to run*
vertically to drain the grease.

Kitchen Exhaust Systems Inspection Sheet

Date of Inspection: _____

Property Inspected: _____ System Inspected: _____

Property Address: _____

Phone: _____ Owner: _____

Appliances

Main Fuel Type: Natural Gas Electric Solid Fuel   Cooking Volume: Very High   High   Medium   Low

Main Cooking Style of this system: Oriental   Deep Fat Frying Griddle   Char Broiling Other: _____

Does exhaust hood capture all heat and cooking effluent?   Yes   No   Gas Shut Off accessible Yes   No

Exhaust System

Hood Type: Filter   Modular Extractor   Water wash   Other:_____

Duct Type: _____ Number of floors of system: _____ Feet of Horizontal Duct: _____

Fan Type: Upblast   In-line   Utility   Other: _____ Fan Termination: Wall   Roof

Entire system interior accessible?	Yes No N/A	System is non-compliant (see comments)? Yes No
Filters conforming and in place?	Yes No N/A	Water wash hood operational? Yes No N/A
Hood Damper operates properly?	Yes No N/A	Dangerous non-conforming access? Yes No N/A
Clearance to combustibles acceptable?	Yes No N/A	Safe access to fan? Yes No N/A
Fan tippable or interior accessible?	Yes No N/A	Recommended Cleaning Frequency: _____ times per year.

Name of Cleaning Company: _____

Next Cleaning Date: _____   Entire system clean to applicable codes? Yes   No N/A

Portable Extinguishers

Portable Type: _____   Current inspection tag (within last 12 months)? Yes No

Gauge in proper range (green)?   Yes   No   Visually in good shape and properly installed? Yes No

Fixed Pipe Suppression System

Manufacturer and Type: _____   Visually inspected (see comments below)? Yes No

Fire suppression nozzles clear/capped? Yes No   Minimum one nozzle for each appliance? Yes No

Current Fire Suppression tag? Yes No   Gauge or indicator in proper range (green)? Yes No

Tamper seal in place? Yes No   Manual Pull accessible? Yes No

Name of Fire Suppression Service Company: _____

Summary

Inaccessible areas exist in this system? Yes No   **Areas not inspected are listed in Comments**

Photos or additional information attached? Yes No   Re-inspection date: _____

Other Components and Comments:_____
_____

This Inspection Sheet is notification of the present condition of the above kitchen exhaust system. It does not include any inspection of fixed pipe or other fire suppression systems. This is **not** a complete list of all NFPA #96 Standards or any local Fire Regulations. Complete references should be consulted if further details are required. Visual inspection only, no mechanical readings or evaluations were taken unless otherwise stated. Errors and Omissions Omitted.

Inspectors Name: _____ Certificate #: _____ Signature: _____

Job Contact Signature: _____ Position: _____

The Kitchen Exhaust Inspection Sheet

The **Kitchen Exhaust Inspection Sheet** will assist in providing concise and accurate information. It also notes needed improvements and other related information.

These may include:

- The need for greater access
- Inadequate, unsafe access panels
- Recommend Construction changes
- Grease buildup on the roof
- Recommend cleaning frequency

Inspection Sheet Format

This form is divided into sections as follows:

- **Establishment Information:** provides details of the site owner and the system inspected
- **Appliances:** Information on the fuel source, type and volume of cooking
- **Exhaust System:** Provides a description of the entire exhaust system and documents the outcome of the inspection along with needed recommendations
- **Portable Extinguishers:** Lists the type and condition of the portable fire extinguishers
- **Fixed Pipe Fire-Extinguishing System:** Lists the type and condition of the fire-extinguishing system

Make three copies of the completed Inspection Sheet:

- One to the inspected establishment
- One for your file
- One to be made available to other departments or agencies

Inspection Sheet Explanation

No form can cover all contingencies. The Inspection Sheet represents a consensus from a number of experts regarding the most important factors in kitchen exhaust safety.

Note: Applicable NFPA 96 and International Mechanical Code References are quoted and paraphrased. Refer to NFPA 96, 2011 Edition, and IMC, 2006 Edition, for exact quotations. This and other forms are available free at www.philackland.com

Legend: N/A = Not available for inspection, perhaps the exhaust system does not have this item.

During the inspection, if you encounter any **"no"** answers or need additional space to describe the system's condition, either use the **Comment** area provided near the bottom of the form or use additional paper.

A rather unbelievable adaptation to the exhaust duct. This material would not last seconds in a fire.

Establishment Information

Date of Inspection: _____

Property Inspected: _____ System Inspected: _____

Property Address: _____

Phone: _____ Owner: _____

Date of Inspection: Enter the date.

Property Inspected: This should be the name of the specific commercial kitchen inspected.

System Inspected: The name of the specific system inspected (if applicable), such as: charbroiler system of main kitchen.

Property Address, Phone: These should be for the location inspected.

Owner: For clearer reference put the name of the head office (in the case of chains), property management companies, or government.

A gas quick coupler and retaining cable to ensure the appliance stays reasonably stationary

Appliances

Appliances
Main Fuel Type: Natural Gas   Electric   Solid Fuel   Cooking Volume: Very High   High   Medium   Low
Main Cooking Style of this system: Oriental   Deep Fat Frying   Griddle   Char Broiling   Other: _____
Does exhaust hood capture all heat and cooking effluent?   Yes   No   Gas Shut Off accessible   Yes   No

Main Fuel Type: gas, or solid fuel: Check **all** of the various sources of fuel used in the cooking line. This will generally mean more than one; be sure to note solid cooking fuels.

Cooking Volume: very high, high, medium, low: The amount or volume of cooking taking place that will contribute to determining the frequency of cleaning.

Main Cooking Style: What is the nature of the cooking creating the greatest grease buildup? For example: a cooking-line of a convection oven, fat fryer, grill and charbroiler – under equal usage the charbroiler would, by far, contribute the most grease buildup. It may be necessary to circle more than one to get a clear picture.

Does the exhaust hood capture all heat and cooking effluent? In commercial kitchens with canopy hoods, all appliances should be under the hood. In commercial kitchens utilizing galley hoods, the fan must have sufficient velocity to pull all cooking effluent into the exhaust system. Any chimney or heat exhausts must be located under the hood.

Gas Shut Off accessible   Yes   No

A grease covered floor behind and under a cooking line that has been removed

---

Exhaust System

Hood Type: Filter   Modular Extractor   Water wash   Other:_____

Duct Type: _____   Number of floors of system: _____   Feet of Horizontal Duct: _____

Fan Type: Upblast   In-line   Utility   Other: _____   Fan Termination: Wall   Roof

Entire system interior accessible?	Yes No N/A	System is non-compliant (see comments)?	Yes	No N/A
Filters conforming and in place?	Yes No N/A	Water wash hood operational?	Yes	No N/A
Hood Damper operates properly?	Yes No N/A	Dangerous non-conforming access?	Yes	No N/A
Clearance to combustibles acceptable?	Yes No N/A	Safe access to fan?	Yes	No N/A
Fan tippable or interior accessible?	Yes No N/A	Recommended Cleaning Frequency: _____ times per year.		

Name of Cleaning Company: _____

Next Cleaning Date: _____   Entire system clean to applicable codes?   Yes   No N/A

Hood Type: Circle type of hood. Is the hood made of anything other than stainless steel? In **Comments**, state if the hood is non-compliant. Hoods shall be No. 18 MSG steel or No. 20 MSG stainless steel, liquidtight continuous exterior weld, and be configured to capture grease-laden vapors.

Duct Type: Shape and condition of the duct (square, rectangle, round, wrapped, non-compliant). Basic requirements are:

Inspectors checking the hood

- All interior surfaces of the exhaust system shall be accessible for cleaning and inspection purposes.

- All seams, joints, penetrations, and duct-to-hood collar connections shall have a liquidtight continuous external weld.

- Ducts shall be constructed of and supported by carbon steel not less than 1.37 mm (0.054 in.) (No. 16 MSG) in thickness or stainless steel not less than 1.09 mm 0 (.043 in.) (No. 18 MSG) in thickness.

Bolted "S-lock" or Pittsburgh seams are not compliant, (NFPA 96, Section 7.5). These types of ducting are not liquidtight and could fail during a fire situation. Additionally, these ducts tend to leak grease when they run horizontally. If these conditions exist, notify the owner.

No. of floors of system: This will assist in determining the magnitude of the exhaust system and the need for access into the ductwork, upper floors and roof.

Amount of Horizontal Duct in m (or in ft): This information will assist in creating a total picture of the exhaust system for the owner, and will help assess the need for more frequent cleaning and/or additional access, as grease will build up in greater volumes in horizontal ducting.

Fan Type: Description of the fan

- In-line
- Upblast
- Utility set
- Other type of fan (explain in Comments)

Fan Termination: Wall or Roof: Confirm that the clearances to combustibles are adequate where the duct penetrates the wall or roof.

Entire system interior accessible for inspection and cleaning: NFPA 96, Section 4.1.8 states: All interior surfaces of the exhaust system shall be accessible for cleaning and inspection purposes.

Inform the property owner of the need for accessibility so that the system can be properly inspected and maintained. In older constructions this will generally require the installation of access panels or modifications to the fan so it is tippable.

Exhaust cleaners have the responsibility to ensure the system can be entirely cleaned, or to tell the owner if it cannot and why, in writing. If they cannot install the necessary panels, have this work done by others, i.e. sheet metal contractor.

Access into the system is paramount to ensure complete cleaning. NFPA 96 requires access every 3.7 m (12 ft), IMC allows for access at least every 3.65 m (20 ft) when the horizontal ductwork cannot be crawled.

Access is required at all changes of direction, such as elbows. Access is also required in utility set and in-line axial fans.

Is there access into the duct above dampers or water wash hoods?

System is non-compliant (see comments)? Expand on relevant issues

Filters conforming and in place: Are the filters in accordance with Chapter 6 of NFPA 96? The filters need to be baffle type: mesh filters are not allowed over grease producing appliances.

NFPA 96, Section 6.2 states in part that grease filters shall be:

- Listed and constructed of steel or listed equivalent material

- Easily accessible and removable for cleaning

- Installed at an angle not less than 45 degrees from the horizontal

A baffle filter with baffles missing. This is a typical sight in many restaurants.

There are many times when restaurant staff will put a baffle filter in <u>incorrectly</u>, with the baffles running <u>horizontally</u>.

A filter installed sideways. Filter baffles must run vertically to drain.

The proper direction of a baffle style filter

Inspection Points – Filter Type Hoods

- Are the filters or baffles clean?

- Are filters seated properly or are they bent and damaged?

- Are there any spaces between the filters?

- The bars of baffle filters should be running vertically <u>not</u> horizontally

- Locate exhaust cleaning certificate

- Have one of the cooking staff remove a filter. With a flashlight, examine plenum chamber and duct

- Check drip tray and trough

- Solid fuel cooking equipment requires special spark arrestor filters

- Is there proper storage of solid fuel or paper product combustibles near exhaust system?

Water wash operational: In most control cabinets, there will be a control switch that turns the wash cycle on manually.

Check the control cabinet to see if everything appears to be working properly. Is there chemical (detergent) in the container? Does everything look connected?

Does the manager know how to turn the system on and off? The manager needs to know this.

If possible, have the wash cycle activated.

Does the water wash system appear to be working properly?

During the wash cycle, the pump should siphon up chemical from the container, (usually located in the control cabinet).

NOTE: *Is there a crystal-like buildup on any of the pipes or connections? Do not touch the crystals with bare hands, as they may be <u>very</u> caustic and very sharp.*

Inspection Points – Water Wash Type Hoods

- Open the door of the hood. Is there grease buildup?

- Are the nozzles spraying properly?

- Is the damper 'Pull' plunger of the water wash system accessible?

- Is the trough draining?

- Is it filled with grease or water?

- Is there a Manufacturer's Service Sheet in the control cabinet? Check to see the last date that the system was serviced. It should have been serviced in the last six months. Most systems are <u>not</u> receiving this service regularly.

A Gaylord control cabinet

- Check that the detergent tank and foot valve are clean

- Check the pump, tubing and pipe fittings for leaks

- Some water wash hoods have removable baffles or cartridges

Water wash hoods and their companion controls are complicated pieces of machinery. A service technician will be able to provide greater levels of inspection and service; have them in attendance during an inspection if possible.[5]

Hood Damper Operates Properly:

- Is there grease built up on the damper or on contact points of the duct or hood?

- Check behind damper for grease

- When the plunger is activated does the damper close properly?

- Check with the cook to see if gas is shut off when damper is closed

- For more, see NFPA 11.3

Remember, when testing the damper it may shut off the gas and the wash-down system may activate. **Always check beforehand** to ensure that the fire-extinguishing system is not hooked into the damper pull control. There are rare occasions when this may be so.

Ask the owner or chef how often they check to see that the damper closes properly. If they do not know (or don't understand) how a damper operates, consult the manufacturer.[6]

---

[5] For more details, see the Water Wash Type Hoods in Chapter 4, Hoods, and the Water Wash Hood Service Technicians section in Chapter 7, Service Providers.

[6] See Chapter 4, Hoods, and Chapter 5, Fire-Extinguishing Systems.

Dangerous Non-Conforming Access Panels: There are still large numbers of access panels that are a serious fire hazard. They may be constructed of thin metal or held on with duct tape or other inferior fastening material.

NFPA 96, Section 7.4.3.3 states that the access panel fasteners (screws) shall **not** penetrate the duct. In the vast majority of access panels, the fasteners <u>do</u> penetrate the duct.

Panels may be of the "slider" type where the access panel slides into a groove in the duct. These cannot be properly gasketed.

If any of these conditions exist the panel must be replaced with UL Listed access panels.

An example of an un-serviced damper. The link will not melt in a timely manner!

Inspection Points – Ducts

- Can all fire-extinguishing system detectors and nozzles in the duct be accessed?

- Is grease visible on the outside of the ducts, especially near weld seams?

- Has grease dripped onto the sub-ceiling material?

- What is the distance separating the duct from the building?

- Access is required at every change in direction of ductwork

- Can you logically and safely see where there is access to all areas of the duct?

- Is electrical cable in or near the duct?

- Are there any paper (combustible) products too close to the duct?

- Are there internal flanges (welds) that could cause grease buildup in the duct?

- Inferior ducting or access should be brought to the owner's attention, in writing

Inspection Points – Duct Wrap

The essential features an inspector must look for when examining an "enclosed" system are:

- Is the system installed in a listed and approved manner where it goes through a firewall or floor? It is important that the system provide the same level of "compartmentalization" as is required by a traditionally rated shaft through a firewall.

- Is the wrap system protected against damage?

- Is the enclosure damaged or torn?

- Combustibles, such as beams or other construction items like plumbing chases and electrical wiring must not penetrate the duct wrap

- It is strongly advised that only solid welded or listed access doors be installed in ductwork encased in these enclosures. Wrap will be compromised if the areas where access panels are installed are not covered with a removable "patch" of insulation.

Wrapped duct with an access panel

- Inspections must be made to ensure the wrap is not being saturated with grease that may be leaking from broken welds in a duct.

Clearance to Combustibles Acceptable: Check sub ceiling for the proper clearance of 452 mm (18 in.) between the duct and wood structures. If not 452 mm (18 in.) recommend insulating materials to protect combustible structures.

> *NFPA 96, Section 4.2.1: Where enclosures are not required, hoods, grease removal devices, exhaust fans and ducts shall have a clearance of at least 457 mm (18 in.) to combustible material, 76 mm (3 in.) to limited-combustible material, and 0 mm (0 in.) to noncombustible material.*
>
> *IMC 506.3.11 Duct Enclosures and IMC 506.3.7.*
>
> *Also see NFPA 96, Section 7.7.2.2.1 for clearances to duct enclosures.*

If you have any questions concerning a particular architectural design, where possible ask the building engineer to clarify.

Note: watch for combustible materials such as boxes and various storage items that may be placed too close to the duct or on top of the hood.

Safe access to Fan: Can a worker safely access the fan to inspect and clean it? This would include being able to get to all areas to either tip fans or remove access panels.

> *NFPA 96, Section 7.8.2.2*: Fans shall be provided with safe access and a work surface for inspection and cleaning.*

Fan Tippable/or Interior Accessible: The vast majority of aluminum upblast fans do <u>not</u> lift off their mounting shoulder. This creates an inaccessible area that cannot be cleaned.

An inaccessible fan

- Should a hinge kit be installed?

- Examine where the wiring goes into the fan.

- Is there enough wiring to tip the fan?

- The electrical pipe (conduit), which generally comes out of the roof and connects to the fan, is a wear point.

Inspection Points – Fans

- Is there a shut off at or near the fan?

- Is the connection between the fan and ductwork according to Code?

- Will the fan lift off the duct safely?

- Are clearances to combustibles maintained?

- Is the roof protected from grease?

Examples of non-compliant access on non-tippable utility fans

A properly hinged fan with a grease containment system installed

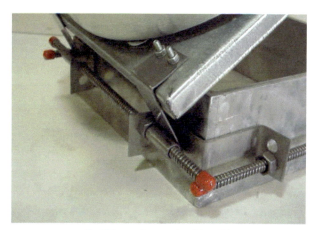

Da Hinge after market hinge kit

Recommended cleaning frequency: _____ times per year: The number of times per year the system should be cleaned to maintain a fire safe environment. Consideration must be given to the type and volume of cooking and the quality of construction of the exhaust system. As an example one national burger chain requires cleaning more frequently based on the number of pounds of hamburger meat cooked translating to more frequent cleanings than every six months.[7]

Name of Cleaning Company: The name of the company that cleaned the kitchen exhaust system.

Next Cleaning Date

> *NFPA 96, Sections 11.6.13 & 11.6.14: When an exhaust cleaning service is used, a certificate showing...date of inspection or cleaning shall be maintained on the premises... (and) ...a written report that also specifies areas that were inaccessible or not cleaned.*

Any areas not cleaned should be noted on the Certificate of Performance. The main reason areas are not cleaned is lack of access.

Editorial Note: The certificate should have two dates on it: 1) the date the system was cleaned and 2) the date the system should be cleaned again. It should have the name of the service company, a phone number, and the name of the certified service person.

A *Phil Ackland Certified* exhaust cleaner should have provided the customer with an *After Service Follow-up Report*. This report should detail any serious deficiencies.

Entire system clean to applicable codes? Is the entire exhaust system, reasonably clean <u>now</u>? The primary "standards" the system should be cleaned to are:

- <u>All</u> areas of the system need to be cleaned to a minimum of 50 microns (0.002 in.)[8]

- <u>No powders</u> are allowed to coat the ductwork

---

[7] See NFPA 96, Section 11.3.1.

[8] See NFPA96, Section A.11.4.2

Portable Fire Extinguishers

Portable Extinguishers				
Portable Type: _____			Current inspection tag (within last 12 months)?	Yes No
Gauge in proper range (green)?	Yes	No	Visually in good shape and properly installed?	Yes No

Portable Type: There are a number of different manufacturers and types of portables. Confirm that the portables are appropriate for the type of cooking that is taking place.

Extinguishers shall be installed in kitchens in accordance with NFPA 10, *Standard for Portable Fire Extinguishers*, and shall be specifically listed.

Current Inspection Tag: Portable extinguishers are generally inspected on a 12 month basis.

Gauge in Proper Range: Check to see that the gauge is in the green. If not, it needs to be recharged. A portable that has been used for even just one short burst will need to be re-serviced.

Visually in good shape and properly installed: Check fittings and nozzle outlet for leakage. Is the safety pin in place? Is the unit accessible and safely bracketed in a holder?

Fixed Pipe Fire-Extinguishing System

Fixed Pipe Fire-Extinguishing System				
Manufacturer and Type: _____			Visually inspected (see comments)?	Yes No
Fire-extinguishing nozzles clear/capped?	Yes	No	Minimum one nozzle for each appliance?	Yes No
Current Fire Suppression tag?	Yes	No	Gauge or indicator in proper range (green)?	Yes No
Tamper seal in place?	Yes	No	Manual Pull accessible?	Yes No
Name of Fire-Extinguishing System Service Company: _____				

Manufacturer and Type: Look on or near the control head for the manufacturer's name and model number for the fire-extinguishing system. Is it Wet or Dry Chemical?

Visually Inspected: Fire-extinguishing systems should only be installed and maintained by authorized and factory trained technicians. A knowledgeable inspector without factory training can complete the following inspection. However, only trained and qualified persons should make repairs or adjustments.[9]

Correct position for a fire-extinguishing system nozzle over a salamander/broiler

Inspection Points – Fire-Extinguishing Systems

- Is the fire system clean?

- Are all nozzles properly positioned?

- Are fire-extinguishing system nozzles installed in the plenum and opening of the ducts? Ensure these are accessible, clean and the protective caps are on. Otherwise, they will become plugged with grease and may not function in the case of a fire.

- Do all penetrations have liquidtight seals?

- Is piping or tubing continuous (no breaks or open ends)?

- Is the EMT cable piping clear of grease? **This is one of the biggest problems with fire-extinguishing systems.** The EMT will plug with grease and the pull-cable can become glued down. When the link is activated – the cable cannot move and the system won't activate.

---

[9] For more information, see NFPA 96, Section 11.2.

- Are the "S-hooks" connected to the link and not to the link bracket?

- Is there a caution label affixed to the hood warning against operating the cooking appliances with the exhaust fan off?

NFPA 17A states that on activation all sources of fuel or electric power that produce heat from the appliances shall be shutoff.

- Gas appliances, whether they require protection or not have to shut off

- The shutoff must be manually reset prior to fuel or power being restored.

- Is the shutoff device accessible for reset?

A gas valve that was resting on the floor behind the appliances. Having an aluminum casting, the caustic of the floor cleaning chemical ate a hole in it. Fortunately the grease was so thick and impacted, the gas only leaked out very slowly--Otherwise BOOM!

Fire-Extinguishing Nozzles Clear / Capped: Fixed pipe fire-extinguishing system nozzles will have an aluminum seal or removable rubber/metal cap to protect them from becoming plugged with grease (water sprinkler systems are an exception – they do not have caps). These caps must be in place and free enough to come off with a small amount of force. **Note:** Missing caps need replacement!

If a cap or cover is missing **NEVER** place aluminum foil on it as a temporary measure. If the cap is encrusted with grease recommend cleaning or replacement immediately.

Minimum of one nozzle over each appliance: Are all appliances adequately protected? Appliances have different fire-extinguishing system requirements. Confirm the proper placement and flow rates with the service provider.

Current Fire-Extinguishing System Tag (Certificate): Fire-extinguishing systems must have a tag attached, which indicates the date it was checked. This is required by NFPA 17A 7.3.2.1. Only the current tag shall be in place. The system shall be inspected and serviced in accordance with the manufacturer's recommendations by properly trained and qualified persons.[10] If the date has expired contact the commercial kitchen management.

Gauge in Proper Range: Check to see that the gauge is in the green. If not, it needs to be recharged.

Tamper Seal in place: Confirm that the safety pin and any tamper seals are properly intact.

Manual Pull Accessible:

Fire-extinguishing system manual pull station with proper tag

- Check the location of manual release for the fire-extinguishing system.

- Are safety seals and pins in place?

- Ensure the manual pull station is not obstructed. Ask staff if they know the location of the manual pull. Ask if they know how to use the manual pull.

Instructions for manually operating the fire-extinguishing system shall be posted conspicuously in the kitchen and shall be reviewed periodically with employees by the management. This should be done when the fire-extinguishing system is being serviced.

Fire-Extinguishing System Service Company: List the name of the company servicing the fixed pipe fire-extinguishing system.

---

[10] See NFPA 96 11.2.1 and 11.6.5

Summary

Summary				
Inaccessible areas exist in this system?	Yes	No	**Areas not inspected are listed in Comments**	
Photos or additional information attached?	Yes	No	Re-inspection date: _____	
Other Components and Comments: _____				
_____				
Inspectors Name: _____ Certificate #: _____ Signature: _____				
Job Contact Signature: _____ Position: _____				

Inaccessible areas exist in this system? The expression "inaccessible area" is usually considered to be where grease cannot be removed. This is particularly true of long horizontal runs of ductwork. If inaccessible areas do not allow for access panels to be installed, an inspector must confirm that the duct cleaning company is able to use a "Spin-Jet" in the duct for cleaning.

An old fashion "panama" fan located in the hood plenum. This was a wall termination.

Other Components - Air Pollution Control Units

All recirculating systems must be listed and shall be installed and maintained in accordance with NFPA 96, Chapter 9 and 13.

Filter cleaning and exchange must be on a rigid maintenance schedule. Pre-filters will require changing approximately every 1 to 3 weeks. The other filters will require replacement at expanded time frequencies. Consult with the APCU manufacturer for the filter changing frequency.

There needs to be access in the duct for grease removal between the hood and the APCU.

As part of the fire prevention system, these units require a fusible linked damper. The links must be inspected and tested every 6 months.

The system owner must have a signed Maintenance Contract with an authorized service company.

Caution: Extreme care must be taken to avoid damaging the cells. Do not grip or push on the cell plates or the ionizer wires.

Inspection Points – APCU

- Open the filter chamber door and remove the pre-filter or first set of bag filters. With a flashlight, look back downstream into the duct to see if there is grease buildup.

- Check that all the filters are in place and clean. Check the fan for cleanliness. If there is buildup, the filters are probably not being changed often enough.

- Open access between the hood and the APCU and inspect the duct interior

Other Components - Recirculating (Kiosk or Ventless) Systems

- Recirculating systems must be listed and operated, inspected and maintained in accordance with the manufacturer's instructions

- Only approved cooking appliances can be used under the recirculating system. A list of approved cooking appliances must be maintained at the system.

- The system must be equipped with an approved damper. The actuation of the damper shall be a maximum of 190°C (375°F).[11]

---

[11] NFPA 96, Section 13.2.10

- The location of the system shall be approved by the AHJ

- Covers (especially over deep fryers) shall not interfere with the operation of the fire-extinguishing system

- Cleaning and maintenance must be conducted in accordance with the manufacturer's instructions. A signed and dated log shall be maintained and available to the AHJ.

- The back of the unit should contain a compartment with the maintenance schedule

The roof under a utility fan with a badly leaking access panel

Other Components -- Comments

List any other components found in Comments

Areas <u>not inspected</u> are listed in Comments: There may be times when you are not able to access areas because of security reasons or other factors. Those areas you are not able to inspect must be noted to ensure that the owner understands the limitations of your report.

Other Components -- Non-Compliant Issues: Some of the most common non-compliant issues are (explain further in Comments):

- Inadequate or non-operational fire-extinguishing system

- Infrequent or inadequate grease removal (Cleaning)

- Dampered hoods with no access into the throat of the ductwork

- Insufficient access in ducts resulting in large amounts of grease accumulation

- Fans permanently attached (impossible to access) to the ductwork and/or roof

- Grease buildup on the roof surface

- Water wash hoods which no longer function

- Inadequate or insufficient filters

- Inadequate clearances-to-combustible because of unsafe food/container storage

- Changing construction requirements

- Deterioration of building and/or system due to aging

- Deterioration of fans and access panels

Photos or Additional Information Attached: If you take photographs, be sure to properly identify them. If you used additional paper be sure to identify, date and initial each page.

Re-inspection Date: When should the system be re-inspected?

Comments: All **No's** or other items are explained in **Comments.** A few Comment examples:

- Condition of the fire-walls and floors

- Size of needed access panels

- Some other component of the exhaust system is inadequate or damaged such as: Roof protection system or Hinge kits required

- Non-conforming hoods or ducts

- Air Pollution Control Devices

Questions to Ask Service Providers

To achieve the best performance from exhaust and fire-extinguishing system servicing contractors, ask the following questions:

To Water Wash Hood Service Contractors:
1) Is the wash cycle operating properly?
2) Did you close the damper and confirm that there is no grease obstructing the seal?
3) Is the damper interfaced with the fire-extinguishing system?

To Fire-Extinguishing System Service Contractors:
1) Have them show you the old, changed links from the system.
2) Are all the nozzles clear and are they capped properly?
3) Are your contractors factory trained and authorized to do this particular system?
4) Are you using factory authorized parts?
5) Is the suppression systems up to UL 300 or ULC 1254.6?

To Exhaust Cleaners:
1) Did you remove the grease from the <u>entire</u> system NFPA 96, Section 8-3.1 (1998) or 11.4. (2011)?
2) How are you cleaning under the fan?
3) Where are access panels located? Are you removing them?
4) Are they properly gasketed?
4) Do you know the NFPA 96 requirements for proper access panel installation?
6) Do you pin off the fire suppression system? **They should NOT be doing this!**

To Restaurant Owners and Senior Kitchen Staff:
1) Do you know where the suppression Manual Pull is and how to operate it?
2) On Water Wash hoods -- Does staff know how to operate the damper control?
3) Does the staff check and refill the chemical tank of the water wash hood?

Require all contractors to provide the restaurant with a detailed written report, in addition to a service tag, of what was done and not done to their system. Require the written report be kept on the premises for your review.

Building Inspectors: Before issuing an Occupancy permit, require a copy of the Initial Inspection Checklist for water wash hoods, suppression systems and any other components that are available. You want written confirmation that these systems are actually installed and operational as designed.

Notify the contractor and/or restaurant that you want to discuss the installation/service they are performing on restaurant systems. This will put them all on notice that you are interested and involved in ensuring the systems are functional and properly serviced.

Inspection After a Fire

In the event ductwork sustains a fire, access panels must be immediately inspected for warping or heat-related damage. If any damage whatsoever is evident, the entire access panel assembly must be replaced. If the panel is not damaged, the manufacturer must be notified so that replacement gasketing can be provided.

NFPA 96, Section 7.7.3.3: In the event of a fire within a kitchen exhaust system, the duct, the enclosure, or the covering directly applied to the duct shall be inspected by qualified personnel to determine whether the duct, the enclosure, and the covering directly applied to the duct are structurally sound, capable of maintaining their fire protection functions, suitable for continued operation, and acceptable to the authority having jurisdiction. Also see NFPA 96, Section 4.2.4.2.

The author inspecting a duct after a fire

THIS PAGE HAS BEEN INTENTIONALLY LEFT BLANK

Made in the USA
Columbia, SC
03 August 2024

39172653R00102